FROM THE BROWDER FILE

22 Essays on the African American Experience

by
Anthony T. Browder

The Institute of Karmic Guidance
Washington, D.C.

3:45

540 992 5905

FROM THE BROWDER FILE
22 *Essays on the African American Experience*

by
Anthony T. Browder

Published by

The Institute of Karmic Guidance
P.O. Box 73025
Washington, D.C. 20056
(202) 726-0762

Cover Design: Tony Browder

Typesetting: Letter Perfect

Layout: Letter Perfect/East Koast Graphics

Library of Congress Catalog Card Number: 89-80061

ISBN: 0–924944–00–5

Printed in U.S.A.
Third Printing

Paperback $9.95

Dedication

From the very beginning, our African ancestors acknowledged the primacy of the female as the source of creation. True to this tradition, I wish to dedicate this work to the creative forces in my life,

My Grandmother, Mary E. Walker
My Mother, Anne E. Browder and
My Daughter, Atlantis T. Browder

Acknowledgements

I wish to thank Zelma Peterson, editor and producer of *Declaration of Financial Independence Radio Magazine*, for her editorial skills and for a gentle nudge when it was necessary. I'd also like to thank Karen Harley for her splendid word processing skills and her ever watchful eye; Greg Thomas, Clyde McElvene and Michelle Taylor for their assistance with compiling the numerous references; Malcolm Aaron for his artistic creativity; Stephanie Brown of Letter Perfect Typesetting Services for typesetting and layout; Frances Murphy, Publisher of *The Washington Afro American Newspaper*, for providing me with the opportunity to create *"From The Browder File"*; Marie Hollis for love, patience and editorial assistance with the early articles; Frederick Jones for his selection of the name *"From The Browder File"*; all the members of the Amenta Study Group for their encouragement and assistance; all the followers and supporters of the Institute of Karmic Guidance; and finally, WOL, WDCU, WPFW, and WYCB radio stations and WHMM television station for allowing me to access their airwaves with this information.

About the Cover

"The Re-awakening"

The cover art represents a "Child of the Sun" coming into enlightenment through the attainment of knowledge. The rays of light, which emanate from the solar plexus, travel up the staff which represents the spine of Osiris, the Lord of Resurrection. This light illuminates the *"Ankh"*, the symbol of life, at the top of the staff. The illuminated ankh radiates light to the pineal gland (the all seeing eye of enlightenment), which is symbolically represented by the serpent on the forehead.

The symbolic imagery of the cover art and the poem *Transition 13*, on the following page, represent the process of self empowerment which comes with the attainment of knowledge.

TRANSITION 13

We knew not
We studied
We learned all there was to know
We taught others

Then we forgot what we had learned
And then forgot that we had forgotten

Now we are taught
(By those who were once taught by us)
Knowledge
(That we already had)

So. . .
We study
We learn all there is to know
We teach others

Will we forget. . .AGAIN

Introduction

By
Asa G. Hilliard, III

Why is it that black people do not work together in unity? Our impaired condition is due to a long-term miseducation process, one that was not of our own making. It should be clear that the remedy for this malady is a **UNILATERAL MENTAL DECLARATION OF INDEPENDENCE.** We must conduct our own critique of our mental diet. We must act as the designers of our own future, based upon a careful and deep study to find the truth about ourselves and about the world. We must establish our own priorities.

We can be led to act in our own interest as a group if we tune into, and add to, our mental diets, the liberating thoughts that are provided for us in *From the Browder File.* No person or group outside of our own is likely to see our need for a collective rebirth of consciousness. Even if they did, they would be totally incapable of acting to stimulate us to take control through independent thought and action. In his *22 Essays on the African American Experience,* Tony Browder not only makes us take a second look, but he also motivates us to establish the rebirth of our consciousness as a personal goal and a group goal.

Tony Browder, by virtue of his model as a thinker, compels all African American thinkers to take a second look. In your thinking and planning, consider the following ten things which African Americans have either surrendered or lost. Consider these things carefully and realize that they account for our overall lack of a sense of unity and direction.

1. We let our names go. The first step towards disorientation is to surrender your name.

2. We have surrendered our way of life (culture). We have stopped speaking the language we knew and we have stopped behaving as African people behave. We have lost our way of doing things and we have adopted the ways of people unlike ourselves.

3. We have lost our appetite because we have lost our names and our culture. Even when those among us recreate our culture and present it to us, we no longer have an appetite for it. We have a greater appetite for the culture of people other than ourselves.

4. We have a general loss of memory. Few of us can tell the story of our people without beginning it with slavery. It is as if slavery was the only thing that happened to African people.

5. We have created false memories. Not only have we lost the true memory of African people, we now have a host of other memories which are totally removed from the truth. Not only are our memories of African people untruthful, but the memories we have of Europeans are also untruthful, and the memories we have about the rest of the world are untruthful as well. In recreating this story, we are not talking about a black history lesson, we are talking about a world history lesson. African people had a major part to play in the creation of the world as we know it. We populated the world and we presented it with its first recorded culture.

6. We lost our land. It now seems as if we no longer have an appetite for land. We lost our land in Africa, and Africans in the diaspora are losing what little land they once held. Anytime you lose your mooring on the land, you lose your capacity to protect your possessions.

7. We have lost our independent production capacity. We have become consumers, rather than producers. It is a shame that we don't even produce something as simple as a "natural comb." We have to purchase combs that are made as far away as Korea. Almost anybody should be able to make something as simple as a little piece of plastic.

8. We have lost independent control of ourselves. We have little or no control of our educational process, our economic situation, our communications, or our politics.

9. We have lost sensitivity. We have lost the ability to perceive when people are doing things to us which are detrimental. We accept inaccurate perceptions without criticism.

10. As a cumulative result of all of these things, we have lost our solidarity . . . our unity. When we lost our unity, we lost our political advantage, economical advantage, and even our mental orientation. We lost a sense of self and a clear sense of belonging. We also lost a clear sense of wholeness, continuity, and purpose.

There is no amount of information alone which can correct all the problems that I've just identified. But a large part of what we must do is to get our memories back in tact and regain our orientation. Only then will other things be possible. Information is power. Read *From the Browder File* and incorporate Brother Browder's thought provoking information into your plan for moving from **DISIN-TEGRATION** to **REINTEGRATION** for our people.

Asa G. Hilliard, III
Fuller E. Calloway Professor of Urban Studies
Georgia State University
Atlanta, GA

Table of Contents

Author's Introduction

I am continually amazed by the ability of words to expand the human mind and open new doors for mental consideration. Everything that we think and know is a result of the information which comes into our consciousness and is stored in our mental computers. This information forms the perspective through which we view reality. It also determines how we function within society, and how others respond to us.

To *inform* means to form or shape the mind or character through study, learning experiences or instruction. The mind, like any computer, is only capable of responding to the information which is in its memory. If the information is not there, you can not draw upon it. If the information is incorrect, then your responses will also be incorrect. The equation is simple; if limits are placed on your thinking, then limits are automatically placed on your ability to view reality and act intelligently.

Educational systems are designed to control the thinking of people through the control and manipulation of image and information. We all are a product of the education that we have received in school, at home and in society. But sometimes, traditional education is not enough, particularly if key elements essential to this education process are omitted.

Many years of my life have been dedicated to re-examining information which was not a part of my formal education. Needless to say, I have learned more about myself and reality than I could have ever imagined. I have come to understand that whatever a person believes, with feeling, becomes the sum total of their existence. I believe that absolute knowledge of self is the ultimate objective of my life.

As I speak to audiences across the country, in numerous lectures, seminars and interviews, I'm often asked, by those who have truly been overwhelmed by my presentations, "How do you know all of this information?" Usually I reply by saying, "Rather than asking me how do I know all of this information, you should ask yourself why is it that you don't know it."

The feelings of *powerlessness* and *misinformation* which pervade the African American community have simultaneously created, in one segment of this community, a real sense of urgency for obtaining accurate information of self. The lack of specific information denies you the opportunity to make intelligent decisions about your life.

This in turn affects the quality of your life in this world and in the next.

Dick Gregory said it best when he stated, "Information is power. Education is not power. Money is not power. Information is power." It is only through the acquisition of information that a group of people can develop the ability to control their destiny.

The current conditions that plague the African American community are a manifestation of a pervading sense of *powerlessness* brought about by *misinformation*. But even under these dire circumstances, a unique form of *karma* is evolving.

Everything in our world is based on the "Law of Karma", which is the universal principle of "cause and effect". For every action, there is a reaction. The popular media campaign promoting "Beautiful babies...right from the start" addresses the relationship between prenatal care and birth defects. This is karma. This is cause and effect.

The same karmic principles apply in relationship to knowledge and information. Despite all evidence to the contrary, we are standing on the threshold of a renaissance of the African American consciousness. This mental rebirth is being spearheaded by the efforts of numerous men and women who are rescuing and reconstructing African history.

We are being shown a new version of history which documents advanced African culture and civilization which preceded slavery by thousands of years. We are now introduced to irrefutable evidence that brings to light the African origins of mankind, the development of the concept of time, the first solar calendar of 365-1/4 days, medicine, law, algebra, architecture, engineering, religion and so much more.

Imagine the effect this new information will have on the minds of school children when they learn that Hippocrates is not the father of medicine, or that Christopher Columbus did not prove that the world was round, and that conceptually it is impossible to discover a land when there are people already living there. These are indeed important times.

It is only through the positive portrayal of the African contribution to world civilization that people, especially African Americans, will begin to see the worth of African people and the necessity of an Afrocentric world view. It is a historical fact that Africans were the first people on the planet, that they developed the earliest civilizations, and that there has been a concerted effort to deny the world of these great truths.

The lack of an Afrocentric world view, in my early education, left me mentally malnourished. The completion of my "formal education" signaled the beginning of my pursuit of seemingly unrelated fields of study which have tremendously influenced my concepts of myself, my people and the world in which I live.

My training as an artist has cultivated within me the ability to perceive information through a profound understanding of symbolic imagery and its effects on the subconscious mind. An Afrocentric view of world history has allowed me to look at myself and America from a totally different perspective. The combined effects of these two methods of knowing are earth shattering.

Allow me to share an Afrocentric epistemological view of this process. Look at the back of a dollar bill. You'll see first hand, the differences between an Afrocentric world view and a Eurocentric view. The symbols on our currency represent the ideology of the "Founding Fathers" and the source of their ideology.

Sharon Bisdee, Keeper of the Seal for the Secretary of State, describes the front of the seal featuring the bald eagle. "It's wings are outstretched, representing dignity, freedom, strength and vision. Above the eagle are 13 stars known as the constellation, which signify that the United States has taken its place among the nations of the world. On the eagle's breast is the shield. The bar at the top of the shield represents Congress. The 13 stripes below the bar represent the 13 original colonies supporting the Congress.

"The eagle carries in its beak a ribbon that displays the Latin phrase *E pluribus unum*, which means *out of many, one*. This signifies that the 13 colonies have become one nation. In its right talons, the eagle grasps an olive branch bearing 13 leaves representing peace.

The left talons hold 13 arrows symbolizing war. The eagle's head is turned toward the olive branch to indicate our nation's preference for peace."

On the left side of the dollar bill is the reverse of the Great Seal. It features a pyramid (comprised of 13 courses of stone which represent the 13 original colonies) and the eye of God encased in a pyramid. According to Bisdee, "The unfinished pyramid symbolizes strength and foundation for future growth.

Above the pyramid, in a glory burst, is an eye inside a triangle which represents the many interventions of "Providence" in favor of the American cause. Above the eye is the Latin phrase *Annuit Coeptis*, which means that 'He has favored our undertakings.'

At the bottom of the pyramid are the Roman numerals for 1776, the date of the Declaration of Independence. Under that are the Latin words *Novus Ordo Seclorum*, (which were suggested by Benjamin Franklin, John Adams and Thomas Jefferson), meaning *A new order of the Ages*."

The front of the Great Seal was designed by Charles Thomson, secretary of Congress; the reverse was designed by William Barton, a specialist in heraldry, and on June 20, 1782, the emblem was adopted by an act of Congress. It has long been suggested that the "Soul of America" is reflected in this Great Seal.

In 1822, a Frenchman named Jean Champollion deciphered the Rosetta stone and revealed the mysteries of the Egyptian hieroglyphs which paved the way for the European interpretation of ancient African history. Today, an Afrocentric decipherment of the Great Seal will also shed new light on the establishment of the United States of American and its relationship with African people.

It is a known fact that the "Founding Fathers" were Freemasons who studied astrology and other ancient metaphysical sciences. Of the men who signed the Declaration of Independence, 51 were masons, as were all of the generals of the Revolutionary War. In addition, 14 U.S. Presidents have been acknowledged as belonging to masonic organizations.

All of the men involved in the creation of the Great Seal were practicing masons who sought to incorporate "specific values" into the symbolism of the new nation. The links between masonry and ancient Egyptian science and metaphysics have been proudly heralded by European masons for centuries. Nowhere is this relationship more clearly defined than in George G.M. James' book *Stolen Legacy*.

James documented the relationship between the Egyptian *Mystery Schools* and the European mason lodges. The word *mason*, which means *child of the sun*, is derived from the African terms *Sons and Daughters of Light* and *Children of the Sun*. The sun is symbolic of enlightenment. Therefore, these metaphors describe the people who had acquired knowledge and enlightenment.

When viewed from this perspective, the significance of the Great Seal takes on new meaning. The front of the Great Seal bears a striking resemblance to the African symbol of Horus (the hawk). The use of this symbol preceded the creation of the Great Seal by over 5,000 years.

Above the hawk is the sun which is symbolic of power and knowledge. Horus is holding in both talons the "shen", which is the African symbol of infinity and above the shen is the "ankh", the African symbol of life. These combined images represent the belief in infinite life, not only in this world but in the next. Contrast this ideology to that of the eagle which carries the symbols of war and peace.

The front of the Great Seal is also replete with the repetition of the number 13. There are 13 leaves and 13 berries on the olive branch, 13 arrows, 13 stripes on the shield, 13 letters in the words "E pluribus unum", and 13 stars in the constellation above the eagle's head. Throughout the seal the number 13 is used 13 times.

What is the significance of the number 13? The logical explanation is that 13 represents the 13 original colonies. But why 13 colonies? Why not 10, or an even dozen? Why not 15 colonies?

In masonic, esoteric and metaphysical literature, 13 is the number of transformation. The completion of a cycle is represented by 12, and

12 + 1 is the transformation of the energy of that completed cycle to a higher, more spiritual level. We see this philosophy expressed in the symbolism of Christ and the 12 disciples, the sun and the 12 signs of the zodiac, King Arthur and the 12 knights of the Round Table, and December 25 and the 12 days of Christmas. There are many other examples.

On the reverse of the Great Seal we find a Pyramid comprised of 13 steps, and above the pyramid we see the "Eye of Horus". History shows that the construction of pyramids occurred in lands occupied by African people in Egypt, Ethiopia and Sudan, as well as by the Africans who migrated to Central America in the 7th century B.C.

The combined use of the pyramid and eye of Horus, represent a clear desire to incorporate Egyptian values in the founding of this nation. A translation of the Latin words surrounding these two symbols further reinforces this point.

Novus Ordo Seclorum represents the establishment of a *New Secret Order* which was founded on Ancient esoteric principles. *Annuit Coeptis* means that God has favored this undertaking and has blessed it with *Annual endowments of unlimited wealth.*

Although the Eurocentric view was that America became great because of "God's blessings", in reality this country emerged as an economic world power because of 400 years of **free slave labor.**

The history of this nation is truly unique. America is the only world power established on African principles. African people were enslaved and forced to build this country in order to bring these principles into manifestation. Suffice it to say, without either of these two components, this nation would not be what it is today.

There are numerous examples of the African influence interwoven into the fabric of the United States of America. The prevalence of these examples is evident in Washington, D.C. During the many years that I have resided in the District of Columbia I have identified a number of sights, such as monuments, parks and statues, throughout the city, which both architecturally and symbolically *"quietly commemorate"* the African contributions to this nation.

Three years ago I had the opportunity of sharing my research on the "Cathy Hughes Morning Show" on WOL radio, 1450 AM. The "Morning Show", hosted by Ms. Hughes, owner and general manager of the station, is a "drive time" talk show which features stimulating news items, discussions and interviews.

The information presented on that program held both the host and the audience spellbound. Ms. Hughes admitted unashamedly that the knowledge shared on the show was so phenomenal and vitally important to her audience that she invited me to return on the next program.

Since that first appearance, I have been a guest on numerous occasions and have even hosted the show several times. However, it was my first appearance on the "Morning Show" which caught the attention of Mrs. Frances Murphy, publisher of the *Washington Afro-American* newspaper.

I was approached by Mrs. Murphy to write an article on one of the topics that I had discussed on the show, the origins of the word *negro*. That first article, *The creation of the negro*, led to a bi-weekly column entitled *From the Browder File*. The collection of essays in this book were written over a two year period and published in my newspaper column.

The information contained in this book is designed to touch your consciousness in a special way and thereby stimulate thoughtful and meaningful discussions with friends, relatives and associates. I have also included references which will assist you in investigating certain subjects in greater detail. I certainly hope you will do so.

We must be every mindful of the fact that just one hundred and fifty years ago, African Americans were still slaves. By law, we were forbidden from learning to read or write. The reasons were very obvious. *"Information is power."* Information holds the key to freedom from mental and physical bondage.

If you deny any people the knowledge of their history and culture, you deny them the ability to develop to their full potential. *"Information is power."* We must be ever mindful of the fact that the short time we have here on earth, provides us with a lifelong opportunity to gather information and use it to improve the quality of our lives.

It is the responsibility of every adult to know their history and culture, to preserve it and then pass it on to the next generation. The youth have the responsibility of using that knowledge, assuming their rightful place in history and then passing this information on to the next generation. This is an obligation, not a luxury. *"Information is power."* Information provides you with the food for thought necessary to *"Free Your Mind"*....use it!

Anthony "Tony" Browder
December 21, 1988

Preface
How to use this book

Information has the ability to inspire you, to make you excited and give you the strength and courage to complete many difficult tasks in life. All the things that I will share with you, you already know. The only thing that I am doing, through the presentation of material in this book, is jogging your mind.

Everything that you need to know, everything that there is to know, is already ingrained within your memory banks. It's simply a matter of creating the proper mental attitude, tapping into that source of information, and allowing the answers to come *through* to you.

The process for personal development as outlined in *Stolen Legacy* was referred to as the "Ten Virtues." The first three virtues are of primary importance; they are 1) Control of thought; 2) Control of action and 3) Steadfastness (fortitude).

The control of your thoughts allows you to select from myriad ideas which will determine your course of action. Life is indeed a trip, and how well you plan for that trip determines how fast and in what condition you will reach your destination.

All of the things that you do in life, your actions, are a direct result of the choices you make through your thought processes. Steadfastness (fortitude) is the ability to chart and maintain a steady course in life.

The essays in this book are presented as roadmaps. These guidelines can direct your thinking in a progressional manner which will ultimately lead to self awareness and self determination.

We begin with the question, "Who are you?" What was *"The creation of the negro"*, and how has that creation affected you and your thinking? Next we examine the primacy of the African as *"The mother of mankind"*, and the impact of that reality.

We go on to restore dignity to *"blackness"* and the black man and woman in America by presenting insightful information "On the Color Black." A positive attraction to blackness leads to the desire to identify with African American *"He-roes"* and *"She-roes"* and to the resurrection of the African spirit.

The ability to identify with an ancestral legacy establishes the capacity to recognize and confront the problems of the present and the future. A firm foundation is always required for the building of any superstructure, and the deeper the foundation, the taller and firmer that structure will stand.

With the historical references firmly established, the remaining essays in this publication will allow you to examine some of the most pertinent issues facing us today from a much broader perspective. Then comes the hard part. That is, the integration of this *"new"* information into your daily life.

Without a doubt, melanin is one of the most important topics to be discussed during the 21st century. We must begin **NOW** to understand the critical issues concerning the psychological and spiritual attributes of melanin and the role it will play in the survival of the "Hue-Man" race.

We must begin today to prepare for our future. Now is the time to start building your "Ark". You don't want to wait until the rains come before you begin thinking about survival.

A good set of blueprints is always necessary for the development of any project, and I would like to offer you a set of working plans. There are seven suggestions that I strongly recommend you consider and factor into your daily routine.

1. You have to begin to unlearn all that you have learned. If you have been miseducated, as Carter G. Woodson stated in *The Miseducation of the Negro,* then you have to unlearn everything that you have been taught. Next you must fill that empty void with accurate knowledge and information.

2. As you go through this process of exposing yourself to new information, you'll have the tendency to get excited and to have a sort of "natural high." You'll want to run out and share this knowledge with friends and loved ones. You can't convert everyone. People will grow when it is time for them to grow. In the meantime, you love them, you appreciate them and you help them when you can. The whole purpose of this information is to reshape your thinking and to increase your potential for good.

3. Once you begin to integrate this information into your daily activities, your life will become an example for others. When you do the right thing, then good will come to you. You must constantly affirm the "Principles of Karma" in your life.

4. Attune yourself with nature and your environment. You must be conscious of the things that go on around you and their effect on you mentally, physically and spiritually. By increasing your level of sensitivity and awareness you will be able to get through times of stress and strain and keep your soul intact.

5. Understand the significance of melanin. This is a gift from the Creator, which serves to protect the body and makes communication with higher levels of consciousness possible. This is a blessing and we are blessed people. It's important that we know who and what we are. It is also important that we do those things necessary to maintain and enhance these blessings.

6. Learn the benefits of fasting and meditation. Positive attributes are available through the regular practice of these two activities. You are a product of what you eat and think, and your body responds to both. So therefore, it is important to monitor what you put into your body, as well as what you put into your mind.

7. Manifest the creative potential that exists within you; it is the source of all power and your key to life. You must also continue to use this creative energy on a regular basis, for if you don't you will surely lose it.

Enough said. If nothing more is accomplished, I would like to think that the essays contained in this book will make you stop and think about yourself and how to exercise greater control over your life through the acquisition and utilization of good information. Look at it this way. The quality of your life is determined by how you use this information...use it wisely.

Malcolm Aaron

The Creation of the Negro

Pick a name, any name – *negro, colored, black* or *African American*. Call a people by any name and they are still the same people, right? Wrong!

The name that you respond to determines the amount of your self worth. Similarly, the way a group of people collectively respond to a name can have devastating effects on their lives, particularly if they did not choose the name.

Asians come from Asia and have pride in the Asian race. Europeans come from Europe and have pride in European accomplishments. Negroes, I am to assume, come from **Negroland** – a mythical country with an uncertain past and an even more uncertain future. Since **Negroland** is a myth, where did the myth of the negro originate? The key to understanding what a negro is, is to understand the definition of that word and its origin.

The word **negro** is Spanish for *black*. The Spanish language comes from Latin, which has its origins in Classical Greek. The word **negro**, in Greek, is derived from the root word **necro**, meaning dead. What was once referred to as a physical condition is now regarded as an appropriate state of mind for millions of Africans now residing in America.

Historically, when the Greeks first traveled to Africa 2,500 years ago, the Egyptian civilization was already ancient. The Great Pyramid was over 3,000 years old and the sphinx was even older. Writing, science, medicine and religion were already a part of the civilization and had reached their zenith.

The Greeks came to Africa as students to sit at the feet of the masters, and to discover what Africans already knew. In any student/teacher relationship the teacher can only teach as much as the student is capable of understanding.

Egyptians, like other Africas, understood that life existed beyond the grave. Ancestral worship is a way of acknowledging the lives of the people who have come before you, and their ability to offer guidance and direction to the living. Temples were designed as places where the ancestors could be honored, and holidays (Holy Days) were the days designated to do so.

The Egyptians had hundreds of temples and hundreds of Holy Days to worship their ancestors. The Greeks thought the Africans had a preoccupation with death. The act of ancestral worship became known as **necromancy**, or *communication with the dead.*

The root word **necro** means *dead.* Another word for necromancy is magic — that *Old Black Magic* which was practiced in ancient Africa. When the Greeks returned to Europe, they took their distorted beliefs with them and the word *negro* evolved out of this great misunderstanding.

Less than 300 years after the first Greeks came to Egypt as students, their descendants returned as conquerors. They destroyed the cities, temples and libraries of the Egyptians and claimed African knowledge as their own.

Not only was the African legacy stolen, but the wholesale theft of African people soon followed. With the birth of the slave trade, it became necessary to dehumanize Africans and devalue their historical worth as a people in order to ensure their value as slaves.

So there you have it, the *negro* – a race of dead people with a dead history and no hope for resurrection as long as they remained ignorant of their past. This was a triple death — the death of the mind, body, and spirit of the African people.

It was strictly forbidden for *negro* slaves to learn to read or write. Such knowledge was the key to liberation and was placed firmly out of reach. As *negroes* became educated, however, they sought to redefine themselves.

The evolution of the *negro* from colored, to black, to African American represents a progression of self consciousness. As a *free people,* we have a responsibility to educate ourselves and rediscover our African identities. Knowledge of self is the key to unlocking the door to the future. The sooner we understand that fact, the sooner we will be able to say *thank God we are an African people.*

References

Diop, Cheikh Anta, *African Origin of Civilization: Myth or Reality*, New York, NY, Lawrence Hill, (1974).

James, George G.M., *Stolen Legacy*, San Francisco, CA, Julian Richardson, 1976.

Williams, Chancelor, *The Destruction of Black Civilization*, Chicago, IL, Third World Press, 1976.

The Mother of Mankind

As 1986 came to a close, a new door in world history was opened. This newly opened door could lead to greater understanding of humanity and mankind, if it is recognized as such.

The sign on the door is rather simplistic, but its significance must be recognized as very profound. It reads: **All Family Trees Lead To An African.**

About 200,000 years ago there lived one woman who was the maternal ancestor of every human being on this planet. This was the conclusion reached by a team of biologists at the University of California, at Berkeley. They reached this conclusion after analyzing special genes in the cells of people from all the world's major racial and ethnic groups.

What this means is that all people of the world are of African descent. This is a claim that the late African scholar Cheikh Anta Diop and European anthropologist George Leakey, have stated for years.

Now that this theory has been "proven" by the scientific community, it can be regarded as truth. The truth is that the first humans came from the Great Lakes region of central Africa. From there they migrated to all four corners of the earth and evolved into the various races of mankind.

The term human can be divided into two basic words, **hue** and **man**. This literally means "man from the humus" (soil, the earth) – a fancy way of saying Black man or man of color (hue). Mankind is composed of the words **man** and **kind**, which describes the *kinds of man* that evolved from **human.**

Basic genetics states that **all colors** are contained within melaninated or dark cells and that white cells contain no color. Simply put, it is possible for a race of brown, yellow and white people to be produced from the cells of black people. But, it is impossible for a race of black people to be produced from the cells of brown, yellow or white races of people.

All the early references speak of man as coming from the earth. Adam, the Biblical first man, is a word which means "Man of the earth." The original name for Egypt was Kemit, which means "people of the Black land." The ancient Kemetian word **Africa** literally meant the "birthplace" of humanity.

Malcolm Aaron

As late as the mid 1600's the entire continent of Africa was called **Ethiopia** – a Greek word which meant *sun-burnt* or *dark-skinned people*. This definition gives new meaning to Psalm 68:31, "Princes shall come out of Egypt (the land of the Blacks); Ethiopia (the land of the sun burnt people) and shall stretch forth her hands unto God." Science has now proven that an African woman has stretched forth her hand unto the world.

The question is often asked, "If the first humans originated in Africa, and all other people descended from an African source, how did the different races of people evolve?" The late Senegalese scientist, Cheikh Anta Diop, discussed this phenomenon in his book, *Two Cradle Theory of Civilization*. He explained that as Africans migrated down the Nile, out of Africa, and into Europe, populating various regions of the world, they experienced profound physical and psychological changes as a result of changes in climate and environment.

These physical changes evolved over thousands of years. For example, in a warm, tropical environment, skin cells are darker to protect the body from the harmful ultraviolet rays of the sun. Hair is naturally curly and short to cool the scalp and protect the brain from overheating. Noses and lips are broad to take in the warm and humid air.

However, in a cold environment where there is less sunlight, skin cells become lighter in color. Since the sun's rays are blocked by heavy clothing worn to protect the body from cold weather, the skin becomes even lighter. Hair is straight and long to insulate the body from the cold. Noses are pointed and thin because cold air must be warmed in the nostrils before entering the lungs.

In the South, the abundance of warmth and sunlight produced a very broad selection of food. Inhabitants saw the Creator of the universe as a generous Being and an ally of man. Life in this type of environment was much more conducive to the development of a higher civilization and society. In cold climatic conditions, people saw nature and the environment as enemies to be fought and conquered on a regular basis. They were forced to protect themselves from cold weather, wild animals and, sometimes, each other.

The "Children of the Sun", in Africa, developed a great affinity toward life and their creator. While the Ice People, living in the caves of northern Europe, felt the creative force was something far removed from them.

Diop's theory explains the basic differences between people of the northern and southern regions. He spoke of a "cultural unity" binding all Africans together. Since all people are descendants of the original humans in Africa, there must also exist a cultural bond between all people.

Martin Luther King, Jr. often spoke of a "brotherhood of humanity." But true brotherhood cannot exist in the shadow of ignorance.

Each year during Black History Month, we have a new truth which must be told as a part of our Black (African/African American) History. We now know our history is also a part of the entire world's history.

This is a truth which we should not allow to slip through our fingers. We should hold this truth for all the world to see, that *we are all an African people*. This is indeed Black history in its most significant form.

References

ben-Jochannan, Dr. Yosef, *Africa: Mother of Western Civilization*, Baltimore, MD, Black Classic Press, 1988.

Van Sertima, Ivan (Ed.), *Journal of African Civilizations*, Transaction Periodicals Consortium, New Brunswick, NJ, Nov. 1984.

Welsing, Frances Cress, *Cress Theory of Color Confrontation*, Washington, DC, C–R Publishing, 1970.

National Geographic, Nov. 1985, (Vol. 168, No. 5).

Newsweek magazine, Jan. 11, 1988, (cover story).

On the Color Black

Blackball. Blackmail. Blacklist. Blackmarket.

Have you ever wondered why most references to the color black have a negative or demeaning connotation? It wasn't always that way. The world, as we now know it, has literally been turned upside down. Many things which were once positive are now presented as negative.

African Americans have been programmed to think that black is something to be ashamed of. It's strange that the people who gave the world culture, science, religion and civilization, know so little about their ancestral heritage. All we have to do is study our history and the perceptions that we have of ourselves will change instantaneously.

Black as a color has the ability to attract to it all rays of color and light. Black is an absorber of both light and cosmic radiation. It is one of the most powerful colors in existence. Our ancient African/Egyptian ancestors oftentimes placed black capstones on their pyramids and obelisks because of the powers inherent in the color black. Some of the world's most sacred icons, including statues and other images, reflect the African reverence for the color black. Shrines of the Black Madonna can be found throughout all of Europe. The large block of stone in Mecca called the Ka'bah is a black monolith of extreme importance to the Islamic community.

The facts are very plain. Black has *always* been, and will continue to be, a source of power and influence, as the following list indicates:

a) Solar energy cells are black
b) Dry cell batteries are powered by black chemicals
c) Judges wear black robes
d) Witches and warlocks wear black robes
e) Priests and nuns wear black robes
f) Graduating students wear black caps and gowns; and
g) Chauffeur-driven limousines are often black.

The scientific, religious and social uses of the color black are based on time-tested evidence regarding the usefulness of that color. Black is a generator of energy. Energy is drawn towards black substances where it can be stored for a determined period of time and used as needed.

In funerals, relatives of the deceased wear black clothing to draw the strength and energy needed to pull themselves through hard times. Black as a color does not denote death. In African and Oriental traditions, the color white is used to symbolize death. Mourners cover themselves with white ash as a symbolic gesture of their grief. When a fire dies, all that remains is a white ash. Therefore, they believe when the fire in man dies, white is the appropriate color to represent death. In military funerals, a riderless white horse symbolizes the dead soldier. On Mother's Day, millions of people wear a white carnation to symbolize their deceased parent. Even the Bible makes reference to death riding a pale (white) horse.

White traditionally represents the absence of life. As we see annually, in the dead of winter, the ground is covered with a *blanket of white*. All life ceases until the spring when the snow melts and new life pushes up from the black earth. In the story of *Snow White*, she was revived from death by a kiss from prince charming, i.e., the son/sun, who traditionally is looked upon as being tall, *dark* and handsome.

In ancient Egypt, the god of the earth was represented by a black image of Osiris, who was often called the *"Lord of the Perfect Black."* As a matter of fact, the original name for Egypt was **Kemit**, which literally meant *The Black Land.* The ancient Kemetians, who are regarded as the fathers and mothers of civilization, referred to themselves as *The Black People.* This was written in hieroglyphic form as a person (or persons) standing next to a piece of charcoal.

The way we perceive blackness has changed drastically over the past 6,000 years. What once was good is now thought of in a negative light. The negative distortion of blackness even applies to the foods that we eat. Think about it the next time you eat a slice of devil's food cake; it is black. Angel food cake, on the other hand, is as white as the driven snow. We must eliminate the idea in our minds that black represents evil and white represents good.

To redirect our thinking, we must first recognize the need for a change. The first steps toward change begin in our minds. Change your mind, and believe that black represents life and power. Reinforce that thought with historical evidence and it will be accepted as reality.

Black is indeed beautiful.

References

ben-Jochannan, Dr. Yosef, *Black Man of the Nile*, New York, NY, Alkebu-lan Books, 1981.

King, Dr. Richard, *Ureaus, The Journal of Unconscious LIfe* magazine; see article *Black Dot The Black See of Humanity*, Winter Solstice Issue (Vol. 2, No. 1), Los Angeles, CA, Aquarian Spiritual Center, 1980.

Jackson, John G., *Man, God and Civilization*, Secaucus, NJ, Citadel Press, 1972.

This is My Country

This is My Country

"Some people think
That we don't have the right
To say . . . 'This is my country'
Before they give in
They'd rather fuss and fight
Than say . . . 'This is my country'
But I've paid 300 years or more
Of slave driving sweat and whips on my back
'This is my country'"

These words were written by Curtis Mayfield in the late 1960's, and they reflected a new attitude which was evolving in the minds of many African Americans. Slavery was no longer being looked upon as a period of disgrace, but as a period of investment.

Black Folk had invested their lives, whether they wanted to or not, in the development of the United States of America. It was the slave who was responsible for making America great.

Many blacks have been miseducated into thinking that Africans were nothing but savages, and that coming to America was the best thing that could have happened to us. In actuality, slavery represents just one page in the encyclopedia of the Africans' greatness.

Many people forget that there was an all-out effort on the part of the slave master to see to it that every positive memory about Africa was erased from the mind of the slave. Memories of thousands of years of productivity were replaced with images of worthlessness. In order to keep a slave a slave, he was made to believe he was worthless.

Even today, 400 years after the fact, many people still believe in the worthlessness of the black race. The solution to this problem, and many others, can only be found if we take the time to know ourselves, and familiarize ourselves with our surroundings.

Take Washington, D.C. for example. Thousands of tourists come here every day to see the handy work of America's founding fathers. These same tourists leave with a greater appreciation for this country, never realizing that were it not for the Africans and their

African-American descendants, this nation would be dramatically different from what it is today.

Consider these facts:

- The Washington Monument (the symbol of America) is the tallest structure in the Metropolitan area; no other structure is allowed to obstruct its view. This is because the Washington Monument was fashioned after an African monument called an *obelisk*, which was symbolic of the regenerative powers of God.

- The design of the Lincoln Memorial was patterned after a temple in honor of Rameses II (constructed approximately 1225 B.C.) who was a pharaoh of the 19th dynasty in Egypt.

- The designation of Meridian Hill Park (aka, Malcolm X Park) was designed to align this city to the same meridian (the pathway of the sun) which passes through Ancient Egypt.

- The layout and design of this city would not have been possible without the assistance of Benjamin Banneker, America's first black man of science.

It is no accident that the so-called *Founding Fathers* sought to recreate, here in America, the same energies which guided and directed our ancestors in ancient Egypt. They utilized African architecture, science and symbolism and removed the African signature. Only a properly trained eye is capable of seeing the truth.

Further attempts to utilize the knowledge of the Africans can be found in the development of Masonry in the early foundation of this country. The Masons patterned themselves after the so-called *mystery schools* of Ancient Africa. Many of the *Founding Fathers* were Masons, as were all of the generals who fought in the Revolutionary War. George Washington insisted that only his Masonic brothers would command his troops.

The links between Masonry and ancient Egypt are irrefutable. Not only are the symbols of masonry derived from Egyptian culture, but so is their name. The word **Mason** (from the latin words *mass* and *son*) means *child of the sun*. The recipients of the highest levels of education in Egypt were also called *Sons and Daughters of Light*, i.e., *Children of the Sun*.

The Declaration of Independence and the Constitution are both Masonic documents which were written in Masonic code and have a totally different meaning to members of the Masonic order. Over the years, the United States has had at least thirteen presidents who were members of *The Craft*.

For the second time in history, the African was responsible for building the greatest nation ever known. This is a living testimony of our greatness as a people, our ability to survive and our ability to create. This is our legacy. This . . . is our country.

References

Woodson, Carter G., *Miseducation of the Negro*, Washington, D.C., Associated Publishers, 1969.

James, George G.M., *Stolen Legacy*, San Francisco, CA, Julian Richardson 1976.

Akbar, Dr. Na'im, *Chains and Images of Psychological Slavery.* Jersey City, NJ, New Mind Productions, 1984

Rogers, J.A., *Africa's Gifts to America*, New York, NY, Helga M. Rogers, 1956.

Rogers, J.A., *Five Negro Presidents*, New York, NY, Helga Rogers, 1965.

Weisse, John A., *The Obelisk and Freemasonry*, New York, NY, J.W. Boulton, 1880.

On Becoming a Born Again African

There's an old familiar saying that, "A people with no history have no future." This is a very true statement. In his novel, *1984*, George Orwell presented another very powerful thought when he wrote:

> *"Whoever Controls the **Past***
> *Controls the **Future***
> *Whoever Controls the **Present***
> *Controls the **Past**."*

If the people who control the present control the past, and the people who control the past control the future, this means that for all of us, the present is the most powerful moment in time. The present determines what memories we will bring to mind from the past thereby influencing all future events. Therefore, the present time in which we live is pregnant with possibility.

There was a time when mention of the month of February brought to mind only Ground Hog's Day, St. Valentine's Day, Abraham Lincoln's Birthday or George Washington's Birthday. Today, however, February is popular for the commemoration of **Black History Month.**

I will be eternally grateful for the efforts of Carter G. Woodson; he started **Negro History Week.** I also appreciate the accomplishments of those people responsible for expanding **Negro History Week** into **Black History Month.** Granted, as a result of the changes made to the calendar by Augustus Caesar, this is the shortest and coldest month of the year; but nevertheless, **Black History Month** represents an idea whose time has come.

I'm always amazed at all the new information that surfaces every February. Just think, if **Black History Month** did not exist, we might not have learned many of the facts that we now know concerning our heritage. Unfortunately, some of us wouldn't even miss this knowledge. I mean, after all, how can you miss what you've never had? Of course, this realization should make us all wonder and question just how much of our history is waiting to be rediscovered.

Just as **Negro History Week** evolved into **Black History Month,** the next logical progression is the institution of **African History Day** – *every day*. It was the African, after all, who was responsible for the creation of time. The first calendar of 365-1/4 days, the hour, the minute and the second are all concepts that sprang from the African mind.

We now have the potential to become *Born Again Africans* if we resurrect within our consciousness the African presence within our midst. The same forces which inspired our ancestors to become pyramid builders, physicians, metaphysicians, alchemists, mathematicians and great men and women in general are still with us today.

The oldest story of resurrection is that of the Egyptian God Osiris (Ausar). It is a story that is over 7,000 years old. Osiris represents the eternal spirit that exists within all beings. His symbol, the obelisk, can be found in every major city in the world. Washington, D.C. is the home to the largest obelisk, it is called the Washington Monument. It is the symbol of the United States and represents its driving force. The *Founding Fathers* saw fit to build this country's foundation on African principals and left symbolic evidence of their intentions. Like the Washington Monument, the symbols on the back of the dollar bill (the pyramid and the all-seeing eye) represent an attempt to resurrect African spirits.

African history is alive and well in America. It just isn't presented as African. The first step in becoming a *Born Again African* is to be aware of the African presence here in America. The second step is to use this knowledge as a philosophical base to build upon. This must be done with an awareness of the importance of this specific train of thought:

> *Your philosophy determines your thought pattern;*
> *Your thought pattern determines your attitude;*
> *Your attitude determines your behavior pattern; and*
> *Your behavior pattern determines your actions.*

All of your actions are derived from your thought patterns, which are influenced by what you believe to be true – *your philosophy.* The idea of becoming a *Born Again African* is symbolized in the logo associated with this philosophical thought. The Egyptian Ankh (an African cross which represents the key of life) is superimposed over a map of the United States and represents two thoughts:

1) The African presence in America; and

2) The resurrection of the African conscious in the American population, particularly those of African descent.

The sooner we recreate a positive image of Africa in our minds, the sooner we'll embrace Africa. Once we embrace the *Motherland* and all of her offspring, we will truly reap the benefits of this reunion. Free your mind. Love yourself. Dare to become a *Born Again African* and you will live your life as it was meant to be lived. Happy African History Day!

References

Van Sertima, Ivan, (ed.), *Journal of African Civilizations*, (see article *The African Roots of Christianity*), Transaction Periodicals Consortium, New Brunswick, NJ, Nov. 1984.

ben-Jochanna, Dr. Josef, *Black Man of the Nile*, New York, NY, Alkebu-lan Books, 1981.

Jackson, John G., *Introduction to African Civilizations*, Secaucus, NJ, Citadel Press, 1970.

Bernal, Martin, *Black Athena; The Afroasiatic Roots of Classical Civilization*, New Brunswick, NJ, Rutgers University Press, 1987.

Parker, George, *The Children of the Sun*, Baltimore, MD, Black Classic Press, 1981.

A Time for Heroes

Everybody's searching for a hero. Everybody needs someone to look up to. These lyrics to the song *The Greatest Love of All*, written by the late Linda Creed, express a basic and fundamental human need -- the need to be loved, and more specifically, the need to love yourself. The degree of self-love is often determined by role models who instill a sense of self-worth.

These role models are often referred to as "Heroes." A hero is a person who is admired for their qualities or achievements and is regarded as an ideal or model. Heroes are very important to children, for they are a source of inspiration. This is the purpose of cartoons. Superman, Batman, He-Man, She-Ra and all the others serve as bigger than life role models for children to emulate.

Positive role models help to instill a strong sense of self worth. Children who have been positively motivated usually become well-adjusted adults. One common characteristic of most criminals is a lack of self-esteem, which often stems from exposure to negative role models during their childhoods. Without a doubt, the influence of "heroes" in the lives of children is the essential element in their development.

A hero can be a father, mother, sister, brother or anyone who can make a positive contribution to the life of another person. Children, adolescents and adults can all have heroes.

The origin of the hero is rooted in the African/Egyptian allegory of **Heru** (often referred to as *Horus* by the Greeks). Heru was the child of Isis and Osiris; he avenged the murder of his father (Osiris), who was killed by Heru's evil uncle, Set. Set was the symbol of evil and is the origin of the word Satan.

The battle between Heru and Set is the origin of the classic confrontation between the forces of good and evil (also regarded as light and darkness). Heru was symbolic of the rising sun (the light). Set, on the other hand, was symbolic of the setting sun (the darkness), which is also the origin of the word *sunset.*

In the battle between good and evil (light and darkness), Heru emerged as the victor, when good triumphed over evil. Heru then became the prototype of the "Hero," the role model for humanity. This story is the symbolic origin of good guys wearing white and bad guys wearing black. White is a direct parallel for light, and black is

Malcolm Aaron

the representation for darkness. It has nothing at all to do with race. The story speaks of the eternal conflict between the forces of light (good/god) and the forces of darkness (evil/devil). The conflict is eternal because darkness always follows the light. Heru, therefore, must be ever vigilant.

This story reminds us that we are in constant need of heroes (Heru) to guide us through the darkness which is sure to come. We must therefore maintain the image and power of Heru (the hero) in our minds in order to overcome the negativity of our lives. When this reality has been reinforced, only then will we have a constant source of strength to draw upon in times of need.

This is why heroes are crucial in the lives of developing children, and also important to adults. We as African Americans must determine who our heroes will be, not only for our children, but for ourselves. For too long, the writers of American history have determined who will be our heroes. This is dangerous, for whenever our history is in the hands of our enemy, our heroes will become zeroes. Those people in whom we should believe, those who inspire and uplift us, will be replaced by individuals with little or no self worth.

Since 1968, African Americans have fought to make the birthday of Dr. Martin Luther King, Jr. a national holiday. Deservedly so, for King had a brilliant mind with incredible insight. Since the passage of the King Holiday bill, I have witnessed some interesting distortions of his greatness.

1. The bust of King in the Capitol Rotunda has created quite a controversy because to some, it portrays King in the image of a weak and insecure man.

2. Dramatic portrayals of the life of King on film often show him as indecisive and totally dependent on Europeans for guidance.

3. The constant referral to King as the *dreamer* sends a subliminal message that he was someone who was not dealing with reality (an awakened state).

King was a man of peace -- but he was also a fighter. He was a dreamer, but he also was aware of the harsh realities of racism which exist in this nation. Prior to his death, King was shifting his posture from civil rights to human rights. The image of the total man has been played down. We are currently presented with the image of someone who was *less* than the man that King was. It is ridiculous to think that the same racist system which was responsible for King's death would portray him as he really was, and give the nation a true hero to admire. It is not in their best interest.

May 19 is the birthday of Malcolm X. Like King, Malcolm was also an important hero. Yet Malcolm's memory and his accomplishments have not been embraced with the same enthusiasm. Is this because the image of Malcolm is too powerful and too demanding to portray him as a role model? Why would they portray an uncompromising individual when they can present someone whose image has become that of a weak, insecure *dreamer*? Why provide the strong, powerful image of a hero who can wake people up, when you can present the image of someone who will keep them asleep?

Now is the time for heroes. Now is a time when we must determine who will provide us with positive images of ourselves. We do not have to wait until a person is dead to view them as our hero. There are heroes walking among us today. There are people with insight and direction who can profoundly affect our lives and the lives of our children.

This is the time for heroes. We must embrace our heroes. We must take in all that they have to offer, for the darkness is upon us and it is the light which comes from the hero that will see us through to the dawn.

References

Kunjufu, Jawanza, *Developing Positive Self-Images and Discipline in Black Children*, Chicago, IL, African American Images, 1984.

Rogers, J.A., *World's Great Men of Color*, (Vol. 1 and 2), New York, Ny, Mac-Millan Publishing, 1972.

Van Sertima, Iva, (Ed.), *Journal of African Civilizations*, (see article *Egypt and Christianity*), Transaction Periodicals Consortium, New Brunswick, NJ, Nov. 1982.

King, Martin L., *Stride Toward Freedom*, New York, NY, Harper, 1958.

Malcolm X, *Malcolm X Speaks*, New York, NY, Grove Press, 1965.

Van Sertima, Ivan, (Ed.), *Journal of African Civilizations, Great Black Leaders: Ancient and Modern*, Transaction Periodicals Consortium, New Brunswick, NJ, Nov. 1988.

A Conversation With Dr. King

I had a dream the other night. In that dream I was afforded a rare opportunity to do what could only be possible in a dream. I dreamt that I conducted a personal interview with the late Dr. Martin Luther King.

I questioned Dr. King about the state of the nation, the progress that had been made since his untimely death, and what he saw in our immediate future.

I would like to share with you some excerpts from my dream.

AB: Dr. King, almost 20 years have passed since you left us. How would you describe the changes that have taken place in the struggle for civil rights?

MLK: I feel that the tactics we used in the 1960's would not work very well in today's society. You see, racism is a systematic way of life, and all systems adapt to change. Our protests forced the government to acknowledge our rights as citizens. Then the system changed. Now our people are struggling to hold on to the changes that so many of us fought and died for.

AB: In 1986, the president signed into law a bill declaring your birthday a national holiday. Has that pleased you?

MLK: The idea of a holiday is gratifying, very gratifying indeed. But I truly hope that people remember the things that I tried to do for humanity. I believe that equality of all people must be realized if we are ever to have justice and freedom in this country.

I do have one nagging concern, and that is the constant perception of me as a "dreamer." My life was devoted to change and action – in a conscious state. Dreams, on the other hand, take place when one is unconscious. People need to stop dreaming and start focusing their attention on what is happening around them. It is time to wake up. I made my *I Have a Dream* speech 25 years ago, and I've had numerous dreams since then. Yes, some were idealistic, but others were dreams of a profound change in tactics.

AB: What tactics would work best in today's struggle for human rights?

MLK: I had a conversation with Frederick Douglass the other day on that very subject. We both agreed that power concedes nothing without a struggle. Sometimes a struggle may begin nonviolently, and then turn violent because of the opposition against it.

Today, the U.S. government is supporting armed "liberation struggles" all over the world, and to them it is justified. Meanwhile, our brothers and sisters in South Africa are told to wait for their freedom just as we were told to wait for ours. The time for waiting is long gone. I concur completely with my dear brother Malcolm and his feelings that we must achieve freedom "by any means necessary." You can quote me on that.

AB: Since the latter part of the '80's, we have seen a dramatic increase in racial incidents. Do you think that racism is staging a comeback.

MLK: Racism has always been present, it does not go away. Like a chameleon, racism changes its appearance to adapt to a changing environment. I dare say that racism is as prevalent today as it was thirty years ago, and in some ways it is even worse. In my day, we knew that society saw us as second-class citizens. We formed our own societies, within our own communities, and we respected each other as first-class citizens. Now, most Negro communities are riddled with crime, poverty, drugs and underemployment. There is little self respect and we are still regarded as second class or third world people.

AB: Dr. King, are you saying that the civil rights movement was a failure?

MLK: No, not at all. The civil rights movement was a means to an end. The movement focused world attention on the treatment of the negro in America, and we forced the government to loosen its death grip on us. We gained some breathing room and we were in the process of shifting our attention towards worldwide human rights when I was assassinated.

AB: Dr. King, if you were to give a message to those of us who were inspired by your work, what would that message be?

MLK: I would say this. In the '50's, we sat in at lunch counters, we boycotted businesses and we demanded the right to vote. Today, you own many restaurants, you operate multi-million dollar businesses, you elect your own public officials, but you are not free.

Freedom comes only when people are truly dedicated to liberty. We cannot take one step forward and two steps back and call that progress. Many of our youth today know little or nothing about their history, let alone the struggles of those who lived a generation before them. We've taken two gigantic steps backward, and it deeply concerns me.

People can no longer afford to waste time, they must wake up, wipe the sleep from their eyes, and continue the struggle. I would hate to think that I gave my life in vain. From where I now stand, I know that we will reach the promised land, but when, is the abiding question.

- -

Dr. King's last words echoed in my mind as my sleep was broken by the sound of my radio alarm clock. I was awakened to the tune of Harold Melvin and the Blue Notes singing *Wake Up Everybody*. How appropriate.

References

King, Martin L., *Martin Luther King, Jr.: Why We Can't Wait*, New York, NY, New American Library, 1964.

King, Martin L., *The Words of Martin Luther King, Jr.: Selected by Coretta Scott King*, New York, NY, New Market Press, 1987.

Haley, Alex, *The Autobiography of Malcolm X*, New York, NY, Grove Press, 1964.

Breitman, George, *Malcolm X: By Any Means Necessary*, New York, NY, Pathfinders Press, 1987.

Douglass, Frederick, *Life and Times of Frederick Douglass*, Secaucus, NJ, Citadel Press, 1983.

Free Your Mind,
Return to the Source:
African Origins

**A videotaped exploration
into the history of Black people
in the ancient world by
Asa G. Hilliard and Listervelt Middleton**

Free Your Mind

We are living in an era when many of the myths and misconceptions that have been an integral part of our primary education are being exposed as blatant distortions of the truth. There are several individuals – whom I regard as my heroes – leading the fight for the *rescue and reconstruction* of African history. Two scholars who have profoundly influenced my thinking are Dr. Asa G. Hilliard III and Dr. Ivan Van Sertima.

Professor Hilliard is an educational psychologist. He holds the honorable distinction of being a Fuller E. Calloway Professor of Urban Studies at Georgia State University. He is regarded as one of this country's foremost experts on educational testing and evaluation. In recent years, his specialization in the history of the Nile Valley has gained national notoriety.

In 1976, Dr. Hilliard wrote the introduction to *Stolen Legacy*, a book which documents the Greek plagiarism of Egyptian science, philosophy and religion. In the introduction, he discusses the concept of a *mental slave* as a person totally unaware that his mind is shackled and his capacity for thought is limited by those who control access to knowledge of the past. According to Dr. Hilliard, a mental slave is a greater victim of bondage than a physical slave.

One of Dr. Hilliard's ongoing efforts to eradicate *mental slavery* is to push for the development of an Afrocentric curriculum within the public school systems. This concept of *cultural democracy in education,* which includes contributions of all ethnic groups, is spreading like wildfire throughout the U.S.

Dr. Hilliard also produced a brilliant lecture series entitled, "Free Your Mind, Return to the Source: African Origins." This series thoroughly documents African history and culture from its beginnings in the Nile Valley, to the present. This knowledge has had a great impact on African Americans. We are now *freeing our minds* and throwing off the shackles of mental slavery and thereby increasing our potential for human development. Once you free your mind, you are able to raise your consciousness, which increases your level of awareness and leads to the enhancement of your personal growth.

It is important to note for clarity that the word **consciousness** is derived from the Latin words **com,** meaning *together,* and **scire,** meaning *to know.* Therefore, consciousness means that one is aware of one's own existence, sensations, thoughts and environment.

The Institute of Karmic Guidance sponsors a lecture series which provides a forum for notable speakers – historians, scholars and psychologists -- whose lectures impart a sense of cultural sensitivity which has a liberating effect on one's consciousness. This program is appropriately titled *Free Your Mind,* a theme I borrowed from Dr. Hilliard.

One of our most inspirational speakers in the *Free Your Mind* series has been the noted historian, Dr. Ivan Van Sertima. Dr. Van Sertima was born in the jungles of Guyana, South America. He was educated in London and the United States, and is currently a profes-

sor of African Studies at Rutgers University. Dr. Van Sertima is a literary critic, linguist and anthropologist. This is quite an accomplishment for someone who was told, as a youth, that he didn't have the mental capacity to amount to anything.

Dr. Van Sertima has been honored as a historian of world repute by being appointed by UNESCO (United Nations Educational Scientific and Cultural Organization) to the International Commission for Writing the Scientific and Cultural History of Mankind. This appointment is sure to affect the world for generations to come.

Dr. Van Sertima is well-known as the author of *They Came Before Columbus: The African Presence in Ancient America*. This book documents the presence of Africans on the continent of America (approximately 900-600 B.C.) some 2,000 years before the arrival of Columbus. When *They Came Before Columbus* was first released in 1977, it was greeted with a great deal of skepticism. In the 10 years since then, however, the critics have been forced to acknowledge Van Sertima's evidence as factual.

The truth is, not only did Africans travel to America before Columbus, they also knew that the earth was round. This was hundreds of years before Columbus "proved it." Prior to 1492, Europeans thought that the world was flat and that if one sailed into the west, the ship would surely fall off the planet.

Africans came to this land first and they came as merchants, not conquerors or slaves. They established trade with the native inhabitants and provided them with knowledge of pyramid building and the construction of 15-ton stone carvings. Contrast this experience with that of European explorers who *discovered* new lands and conquered them in the name of European heads of state who financed their expeditions. They showed no regard for human life whatsoever.

Every October 12, this nation celebrates Columbus' discovery of America and no one asks, "How can someone discover a land where people are already living?" To discover something means to *uncover* something that is already in existence. It is a testimonial to the ignorance of the discoverer, not the *discovered*.

Congress is currently preparing for the 500-year anniversary of Columbus' *discovery* of America. This celebration will take place in 1992 and is sure to rival those held for the founding of America, the signing of the Constitution and the birthday of the Statue of Liberty, all combined. Unfortunately, this celebration will honor a falsehood.

Dr. Van Sertima addressed this concern when he testified before Congress on July 7, 1987. In a presentation entitled *Challenging the Columbus Myth*, Van Sertima presented his evidence and questioned the validity of the use of the word *discovered*. He urged Congress to consider other alternatives. Quoting Van Sertima, *"To use the word 'discover' is to insult the Africans who journeyed here long before Columbus, and it ignores the indigenous inhabitants to whom this land once belonged."*

We all have been victims of a gross miseducation which has produced various levels of "mental slavery." Through the efforts of men such as Dr. Hilliard and Dr. Van Sertima, we now have an opportunity to free our minds and enjoy a new sense of self-awareness and growth.

We all must do our part to try to set the record straight. We must begin to use our homes, churches and schools as environments to cultivate this new ideology of cultural democracy.

We are currently standing on the threshold of an important time in history. We are witnessing a changing of the guard at the repository of truth. If we are lucky . . . maybe our children will inherit a world where the history of mankind will be accurately told, and society will be the better for it.

References

Hilliard, Asa G., *Free Your Mind, Return to the Source: African Origins*, (videotape).

Van Sertima, Ivan, *They Came Before Columbus, The African Presence in America*, New York, NY, Random House, 1976.

Van Sertima, Ivan, *Transcript of Congressional Presentation; Challenging the Columbus Myth*, Highland Park, NJ, Legacies, Inc. 1987.

Van Sertima, Ivan, (Ed.), *Journal of African Civilizations, African Presence in Early America*, Transaction Periodicals Consortium, New Brunswick, NJ, 1986.

Van Sertima, Ivan, (Ed.), *Journal of African Civilizations, Nile Valley Civilizations*, Transaction Periodicals Consortium, New Brunswick, NJ, 1986.

Von Wuthenau, Alexander, *Unexpected Faces in Mexico*, New York, NY, Crown Publishers, 1975.

Additional References

Both Dr. Hilliard and Dr. Van Sertima are available for speaking engagements. They may be contacted by calling or writing:

Dr. Asa G. Hilliard
P.O. Box 91123
East Point, Georgia 30364
(404) 762-6604

Dr. Ivan Van Sertima
347 Felton Avenue
Highland Park, New Jersey 08904
(201) 838-4667

Youth's Responsibility to the Future

Black History Month is always a good time to develop greater appreciation for the African contributions to world culture and civilization. It offers an excellent opportunity to relish and glorify the accomplishments of our ancestors, but time should definitely be set aside to make a careful assessment of the status of our youth. After all, Black History Month is specifically designed to provide positive information for black children.

My personal observations, along with published research articles, have disclosed a serious deficiency in our young and their assessment of their history.

1) While lecturing at a junior high school, I was quite disturbed to see a minimum of 12 students ejected for disorderly conduct within a 30-minute period.

2) A survey at Boston University showed that 35 percent of the students thought the late Dr. Martin Luther King, Jr. was either a former entertainer or baseball player.

3) A black history speaker in New York was approached by a student and asked "Just who is this Malcolm 10, and what happened to the other nine?"

These three examples represent just the tip of the iceberg. They reflect a frightening trend that is currently sweeping the nation. Maybe Black History Month has become so trivialized that it just isn't taken seriously anymore.

Personally, I think the problem is one of complacency. Many parents and adults are not fulfilling their obligations of their heritage by seeing to it that our history is preserved and passed on to the next generation.

The disciplinary problems that currently exist within our school systems are not the fault of the teachers, but the parents. I remember, as a grade school student, that one wouldn't dare talk back to the teacher, let alone get out of line. Today, this type of student is the exception, not the rule.

A child's behavior reflects his or her upbringing in the home, in the schools, or in the streets. The fact that so many of our youth disrespect authority figures indicates that they disrespect themselves. Self-respect is a trait which must be initiated and reinforced at home.

For whatever reason, many parents have forfeited their obligations to raise their children along specific guidelines.

While watching a recent segment of *Eyes on the Prize*, concerning Dr. King's use of children in the forefront of the demonstrations, I learned that as many as 2,000 youth filled the jails within one week. Parents were willing not only to put their lives on the line, but also the lives of their children.

This was 30 years ago, but we still find the same strategy being used in South African protests today.

I wonder how many parents in America, today, would be willing to put their necks on the line for the struggle for human rights. I also wonder how many youth would be willing to sacrifice their gold chains, designer clothes and stereos for the same struggle.

Our youth today are not living up to their potential. It is our responsibility as adults to see to it that they get back on the right track. Our youth have the responsibility to see to it that our legacy is carried on. Every generation has the privilege of standing on the shoulders of the generation that preceded it – but it has no right to pick their pockets.

References

Karenga, Maulana, *Introduction to Black Studies*, Los Angeles, CA, Kawaida Publications, 1982.

Kunjufu, Jawanza, *Countering the Conspiracy to Destroy Black Boys*, Vol. 1 and 2, Chicago, IL, African American Images, 1985 & 1986.

Hechinger, Grace, *How to Raise a Street Smart Child*, New York, NY, Crest Fawacet, 1985.

Fulfilling the Need to Know

I've often marveled at the inquisitive nature of a child. I have a young daughter, and every other word from her mouth is centered around a question. Why? How come? Where? When?

Children are born into this world with a natural desire to know. They are bright and observant, nothing escapes their gaze. They take in information and formulate questions based on what they've been exposed to.

Children are natural scientists. The word **scientist** is derived from the latin word **scire** – which means *to know*. Somewhere between grades 4 and 8, many of our children lose this natural "God-given" talent. Their minds become stifled and the door to the path of knowledge is slammed shut.

Since we are all born with a natural desire "to know," if we lose this desire somewhere along the road, we have to find out where we lost it in order to get back on the path. Many people feel that the educational system is at fault. Oftentimes when we're seeking the answer to who is at fault, if we look within ourselves, we'll find that the answer was right under our noses all the time.

We'll find the key to developing effective educational systems by understanding the meaning of the word **education**. The term is derived from the Latin **educere** meaning, *to bring out.* The process of education is therefore the process of bringing out knowledge which is already inside of you. This age-old methodology was first developed and cultivated by our African foreparents in ancient Egypt.

These institutions for learning, called the *Mystery Schools,* gradually introduced education, progressing through varying levels of instruction. Students in educational environments that are conducive to learning will naturally learn more.

Contrast this situation to modern times. Today, people are force fed information that often contradicts what they instinctively know to be true. Imagine being taught that in 1492 Columbus discovered America, when *instinctively* you know that there were people already living here who were fully aware of where they were. It's no wonder that people don't learn!

The mind is like a computer. If you put nonsense in, you'll get nonsense out. Consistently feeding misinformation into a fertile mind causes it to stagnate. This process is referred to as *atrophy*. This is the failure of an organ to grow because of insufficient nourishment.

As a parent, I made a pledge to myself to keep my mind as fertile as possible so that I can provide positive and meaningful information for my child. In order to fulfill her need to know, I must fulfill mine.

Education is a continuous, ongoing process. It doesn't stop with elementary or high school, college or graduate school. It continues until you die. A mind is truly a terrible thing to waste.

In the summer of '74, my first year out of college, I began to realize how much I didn't know. That year, I began my enrollment in a life-long educational program which has allowed me to view my existence from a totally new perspective.

For many years, I have devoted my time to the study of Ancient Egypt and its impact on world civilizations. I have experienced a profound reawakening and appreciation of knowledge and history. As I share this information with children and adults in my lectures and seminars, I see in their eyes, and feel from their hearts a deep sense of gratitude.

There's more to it than that, however. The knowledge of prior accomplishments establishes a link with the past which lays a foundation for the future. Everything is rooted in the past. Knowledge is the common pathway between the two. Knowledge can be obtained at any time.

If I were to suggest a daily regimen for African-Americans, it would be that we rededicate ourselves to fulfilling the need to know. It is our birthright and our obligation to our children.

References

Kunjufu, Jawanza, *Developing Positive Self Images and Discipline in Black Children*, Chicago, IL, African American Images, 1987.

Wilson, Amos, *Psychological Development of the Black Child*, New York, NY, African Research Publications, 1978.

Rogers, J.A., *Your History: From the Beginning to the Present*, Baltimore, MD, Black Classic Press, 1983.

Rogers, J.A., *100 Amazing Facts About the Negro*, New York, NY, Helga M. Rogers, 1970.

Akbar, Na'im, *From Miseducation to Education*, Jersey City, NJ, New Mind Productions, 1982

Hustlers Die Young

During the 20 years since the riots of the 1960's, it appears that little progress has been made in the African American community. Crime is at an all time high. Unemployment is even higher and drugs are tearing apart the soul of most neighborhoods. All of these problems are having an adverse affect on our black youth.

In one of my many community lectures, I asked a group of high school students what their plans were for the future. For those who had given it some thought, the typical response was that they wanted to become a professional athlete or entertainer. But there were a couple of students who had different aspirations . . . they wanted to be hustlers.

This response disturbed me because the likelihood that an aspiring youngster will become a professional athlete or entertainer is slim, but attainable. The key to success is hard work. But a young person does not need a key to become a hustler. All he needs to know is how to pick a lock. Achieving this life goal requires a parasitic mentality.

Those who choose to become hustlers begin their careers by either selling drugs or committing robberies. Both roads lead to quick money, fast living and . . . a dead end street. Unfortunately, there are hundreds of black youth who choose to take this route.

On any given day you can see these teenagers driving Mercedes' or BMW's, wearing designer sweatsuits and eyeglasses, and carrying handbags which cost more than what most folks pay for rent. Where are the parents of these children and why don't they care?

Unfortunately, many of these teenagers make more money in a month than their parents make in a year. I am bothered by the fact that most of these young people have very little regard for their lives and even less for the lives of others. Most are out of touch with anything outside of their immediate environment, and see only those things which bring immediate personal gratification.

It's a shame to see teenagers walking around with hundreds of dollars worth of gold jewelry around their necks, never realizing that most of that gold comes from South Africa. They don't care to know that the South African government exports $50 million a day in gold while black miners die at the rate of 33 a day. They don't realize that they are helping to enslave their own brothers.

Many of these teens are unaware that the most dangerous period in the life of a black male is between the ages of 13 and 25. This is the time period when many youth become disillusioned with school, get involved with drugs, and turn to a life of crime. All these activities contribute to the development of a permanent underclass with little or no hope for improvement for themselves or their future families.

There are very few old drug pushers or thieves. Most die early in life. Those who do survive often wish that they were dead. They live out their lives in the prisons and flop houses of this nation. It is not a pretty picture.

In most instances, people who take a wrong turn in life do so because they lack guidance and exposure. People who become successful, set their sights on a particular goal early in life and continually strive toward it. Those who are unsuccessful cultivate unsuccessful habits early in life.

It is a simple case of cause and effect. We all get out of life what we put into it. The habits we cultivate in our youth determine how we will live our adult lives. Just ask the person who sits behind a desk or the one who sits behind bars. They both got where they are by employing the same methods – one positive, the other negative.

There are no simple solutions to this problem. It is a complex situation which affects us all. Therefore, we are all required to be actively involved in seeking solutions. Our youth are our future. We can't afford to turn our backs on them.

Everyone – parents, educators, businessmen, and others – must become involved and do whatever they can to influence and improve the life of at least one youth. All of our lives depend upon this.

References

Karenga, Maulana, *Selections from the Husia*, Los Angeles, CA, Kawaida Publications, 1984.

Kunjufu, Jawanza, *Developing Positive Self Images & Discipline in Black Children*, Chicago, IL, African American Images, 1987.

Mandella, Winnie, *Part of My Soul Went With Him*, New York, NY, W.W. Norton, 1984.

Arnold, M. (Editor), *Steve Biko: Black Consciousness in South Africa*, New York, NY, Random House, 1978.

Reflections on a Boy Gone Bad

Nature often sheds more light on our understanding of the complexities of human behavior when we examine the fascinating life cycles of some insects. The cicada is an unusual, broad-winged insect whose newly hatched eggs remain buried many years in the ground before emerging as full-grown "17-Year" locusts. From time-to-time, I like to take the opportunity to make public service announcements, particularly when I feel I have an important message to share with my readers. Please allow me to present my thoughts on the "Cicada-like" emergence of Michael Jackson.

If a young child had watched the mother cicada bury her newly hatched eggs, I'm sure the child might wait in great anticipation to see what kind of insect would emerge from the ground 17 years later. Similarly, today I find myself wondering just what type of star Michael Jackson has become and just what type of strange behavior will be next to emerge from his ever evolving personality. In a brief four-year period, his transformation has tainted his image as the world's most popular celebrity. Now, as the world's most bizarre celebrity, his current behavior is indicative of someone who should be taking an extended tour of St. Elizabeth's Mental Institution in Washington, D.C. instead of touring Japan.

Let me begin by saying that, like many of you, I grew up listening to the music of the Jackson 5, which became popular during the early '60's. I remember attending their concerts at the Regal Theater in my home town of Chicago. Even then, Michael was viewed as a child prodigy. The early musical talents he displayed were remarkable and awe inspiring. The young performer had a voice like Jackie Wilson and he moved and danced like James Brown. He was destined to become a star.

His *Thriller* album proved Jackson to be a star of the highest magnitude. Over 40 million copies of this production were sold worldwide. Fans anxiously awaited the follow-up album, released five years later. This album lived up to its name and was literally *Bad*.

Bad was perceived by music critics as falling short of its expectations. The writing was weak and the music was even weaker. All of that aside, the record company and promoters were quite successful in generating sales for both the album and the promotional tour.

Armed with a new book titled *Moonwalk,* a new video, and a new image, the *Peter Pan of Pop* was out to recapture the minds and hearts of the world. But something was missing. I believe that the thrill was gone, and that we must now make a personal decision as to whether we will accept or reject any future offerings by Michael.

After 23 years in the entertainment business, Michael Jackson has become void of any sense of self. He has become obsessed with an age-old mental disorder called *artificial assimilation* – the overwhelming desire to recreate oneself in an image other than one's own. Michael has perfected the art of passing and has given new meaning to the word *crossover.*

By now, everyone is aware of the fact that the boy has physically altered his body through cosmetic and plastic surgery. He has radically reconstructed his nose, reshaped his chin and added a dimple. Jackson's eyes have been tattooed with permanent mascara. His jherri-curl hairstyle, heavily coated with gels and grease, accidentally caught on fire and *thrilled* him with the brief experience of being a human torch.

Now some of you might view these actions as Michael Jackson's right to do whatever he wishes with his body. But the final straw that broke the camel's back was his decision to lighten his skin color through some bleaching process. Now I ask you, what type of person would take injections to lighten his skin at a time when white people are dying of skin cancer by the thousands because they lack adequate skin pigmentation? Are these the actions of someone who is in his right mind? Michael Jackson has literally gone "Bad." Anyone who sells 40 million copies of a single album is definitely communicating with an awful lot of people. Michael's desire to become white is not an accident, it is part of a promotional strategy to

market him to a predominantly nonblack audience. That is a reality that we have to recognize.

Since becoming a world-wide commodity Michael has specifically chosen not to portray the image of a strong black male. Typically, black males are viewed as a threat by caucasians, therefore, a non-threatening image of Michael had to be created. So now we have a superstar who is neither black nor white, male nor female. His image is that of someone who is sexually neuter and void of any racial ethnicity.

Personally, I feel Mr. Jackson has gone too far, many others also share my feelings. His new image is considered a joke. The general consensus among young people I've talked with is that Michael is trying to imitate his sister Janet. Some say he looks much prettier than his sister LaToya. I recently heard a white discjockey laughingly remark that he thought he looked like Michael Jackson, and, with an insulting smirk, he commented, "Well, at least we have the same color skin."

Many of you probably feel Michael has the right to do whatever he wants in the privacy of his own personal life. Most will agree that as an entertainer, his performances are beyond compare. Both statements are correct. However, when a person becomes so popular that he can influence the lives of millions of people, then his image and personal behavior are causes for public concern.

Images are shaped, molded and created by public relations experts. Stars become stars because people buy and support the products created using their talents. The public is responsible for buying millions of records and millions of concert tickets. These purchases make the stars rich. People in the marketplace determine the popularity of stars and famous people. In order for the career of a celebrity to remain successful, he or she must maintain the continued popular support and approval of fans. This philosophy is true for all professions. It doesn't matter whether the person is an entertainer or a politician, they all have a responsibility to project a positive image to members of the public.

References

Jackson, Michael, *Moonwalk*, New York, NY, Doubleday, 1988.

Fanon, Franz, *Black Skin/White Masks*, New York, NY, Grove Press, 1967.

Television and its Influence on African American Children

Recent studies indicate that children who watch a lot of television are more likely to have problems adjusting to society. They are also likely to exhibit characteristics of extremely high levels of socially aggressive behavior. The influence of television on the lives of African American children is much greater than ever anticipated.

While a great deal of attention has been focused on the effects of TV on the average viewer, special emphasis must be placed on the far-reaching effects this form of electronic media has on the African American child. These children watch TV an average of 7 hours per day, as compared to 4-1/2 hours of daily television viewing for white children. This medium, therefore, plays a greater role in developing attitudes and behavior patterns which may affect black youths for many years to come.

The following facts are important to note:

- Black children tend to be more emotionally involved in the plot of TV programs.

- Black children often use TV as a substitute for other activities such as reading or interacting with other children.

- Black children tend to use TV as a source for role models. They imitate other people's behavior, dress, appearance, and speech.

- Black children use information gathered from television for guidance and direction when making career choices.

- TV provides examples for interacting with members of the opposite sex.

- TV is used as a primary source of learning and perfecting aggressive behavior.

- Black children closely identify with television characters — particularly the black characters.

You must realize that television trivializes human life by showing a murder every 57 seconds. This fact impacts directly on the high rate of black-on-black homicide. This is a cause and effect relationship. You should also realize that the high rate of teen pregnancy among blacks is directly related to the numerous programs which feature sexual promiscuity. Few television shows provide information on sexual responsibility.

A 1978 study completed at Michigan State University showed that:

- Black children believed that TV was very true to life.

- Forty-six percent of elementary school children believed that blacks on TV were representative of blacks in real life.

- Commercials are more believable for black children than white children.

- Over 50 percent of all black children between the ages of 5 and 12 believe that commercials present true and accurate information.

A 1975 study showed that most black children believed that when they felt ill, they should take aspirin, Tylenol, Alka Seltzer Plus or Nyquil. These same children felt that if they wanted a healthier lifestyle, they should take vitamins, drink sodas and eat fast foods. Common sense tells you that this thinking will lead to chaos, premature disease and death.

Even though television has been a negative influence on the lives of African Americans, I would be the last person to suggest that you do the impossible and turn off your TV sets! I strongly believe that "the answer to most problems can be found within the problem itself." One must first take a look at a situation and then derive a solution from that assessment.

We must all ask ourselves the following questions:

1. How much time do my children spend watching TV each day?

2. How much time do I spend watching TV with my children?

3. What programs are my children watching and what are they learning from these programs?

Naturally, adults must have good television viewing habits before they can teach good viewing habits to children. It's important that adults become aware of the powerful influence of television and

then develop a discriminating eye. We, in the Washington, D.C. community, are fortunate to have access to channel 32, WHMM-TV at Howard University. We should support that station, and others like it, because it provides us with positive programming.

Now that cable television is available, many of you pay a monthly fee to watch additional programs featured on numerous channels. Have you ever wondered why commercial TV is free? It's because the advertisers pay for the air time and TV programs are packaged around the advertisers' commercials. Commercial messages provide financial support for existing television programs.

Understand that commercials are designed to influence the way you think. Viewers are programmed to be receptive to a particular product. When you are aware of these facts, it's easy to understand why these programs are offered free of charge. TV programs are specifically designed to influence the viewer's thought processes. If you respond favorably to the content of the program itself, then you will be particularly susceptible to the commercial messages.

Much has been written over the years about the effects and influence of television on the lives of the American viewing audience. When you take the following statistics into account, it is easy to see how important television has become in the lives of most people.

- The average American household has at least two TV sets, and one video recorder.

- The average American spends 1/5 of their lives (approximately 15 years) watching TV.

Of the time spent viewing TV, approximately 50 minutes of each day is spent just watching commercials. That amounts to a lifetime average of 1-1/2 years of watching just TV advertisements.

With this information in mind, it is foolish to look at TV as anything other than a molder of minds. TV is directly responsible for presenting the thoughts and images which guide and shape the minds of millions of viewers. So, watch your television with caution, and be aware of its potential mental health hazards, after all, it is you who controls your TV set.

References

Wilson, Amos, *Developmental Psychology of the Black Child*, Africana Research Publications, New York, NY, 1978.

Kunjufu, Jawanza, *Lessons From History: A Celebration In Blackness*, Chicago, IL, African American Images, 1987.

Exploding the Myths

Little Known Facts About Religion

Years ago, as a youngster attending many weekly Sunday school and church services, I began wondering about the truth of religious stories and teachings. I remember my grandmother warning me that if I didn't go to church, I would burn in hell forever, and if I asked the devil for water, he would put fire down my throat, laughing unmercifully while I suffered.

One day, while trying to fathom the concept of eternity, I let my imagination flow and developed some interesting insights. I asked my Grandmother, "Mama, what would you say if you found out there was no heaven and no hell? Never at a loss for words, this deeply religious woman looked at me in shock and disbelief, and responded, "Nonsense! Why there has to be a heaven and hell! It just has to be true 'cause it says so right here in my Bible!"

For my Grandmother, this thought was just too horrible to bear. But like many other "believers," she would never allow any information to come into her mind that was inconsistent with her present beliefs.

Many people do not, and cannot, accept any statements that do not confirm what they presently believe, even if the beliefs that they presently hold to be true are based on false information and are inconsistent with reality. Many of the things that "the mind of man believes, the mind of man has conceived," but these things are not always based on truth.

Years ago, people believed that the sun revolved around the earth and that the earth was flat. This belief was accepted as true until proven otherwise. The earth has always revolved around the sun and it was always round. This is reality. The only thing that has changed is people's understanding of this reality.

You are the sum total of all of your beliefs and your beliefs are always subject to change as your knowledge base expands. Most people refuse to accept a new belief simply because it contradicts their present belief system. To continue to believe in a proven false-

hood is detrimental to the believer. One must never be afraid to evaluate new information and accept it if it is proven to be true.

In light of this fact, we must be willing to evaluate our belief systems, even if this means exploding the myths that have served as our foundation. People fear instability, therefore it is natural for them to resist the destruction of their old belief system until they have an acceptable belief system to replace the old one.

During ancient times temples were created as places of worship and environments for the development and perpetuation of a culture's belief system. When a temple outlived its usefulness, it was dismantled and a new temple was built upon the site of the old one, using some of the same stones as "seeds" for the new temple.

Africans were the first people on this planet to develop a system of religious beliefs. Their temples were repositories for knowledge pertaining to themselves and their Creator. Thousands of years after these religious beliefs had been developed and implemented, they were stolen by foreigners and used as the foundation for the development of new religious systems which spread throughout the world.

I'm finding more and more in my class sessions, and during my many workshops, seminars and lectures for the Institute of Karmic Guidance, that people are seeking answers. They're questioning and reevaluating their religious belief systems. I'm often asked my opinion about the contents of the Bible, and the name of the religious denomination that I hold to be the one true religion.

This is such a sensitive, personal and emotional area, that during the earlier days of my career, I held fast to the opinion of the great leader Malcolm X, who maintained that religion is a very personal and private relationship between an individual and his or her "GOD." This relationship should remain very personal and private. I've tried to stay away from these types of discussions, but so many people have inquired that now I find it very necessary to address these concerns.

There are many truths to be learned regarding the lives of some biblical personalities, but truth seekers must know the history of all the people who were custodians of these stories. Knowing that history, truth seekers must attempt to learn how and why the stories were changed. Only then can the real truth be known.

Two hundred years ago, Napoleon Bonaparte made a very important statement. He stressed the fact that, "History is a lie agreed upon." We must understand that the stories and historical facts have been changed to suit the purposes of the dominating culture.

Once a lie is told, it is often perpetuated. Lies and untruths can be told for so long that they will be accepted as the TRUTH. When someone comes forward and reveals the real TRUTH, people often don't have the mental capacity to accept and relate to it.

The word **Holy Bible** is derived from the Greek words *Helios Biblos*. Helios means sun and *Biblos* is derived from the Egyptian word for papyrus which means paper. Accumulated papers make books. "Holy Bible" means *Sun Book* and represents the knowledge of the "Children of the Sun" as contained in *The Egyptian Book of the Dead, The Writings of Thoth* and other books.

The Bible is the collection of books which Christian people regard as sacred. Here they find the record of the teachings that are the basis for their beliefs. History documents that these teachings are actually derived from the writings of ancient African priests, rulers and philosophers.

Ancient African texts document the first stories of the Annunciation, the Immaculate Conception, the Virgin Birth and the World's First Savior, who was proclaimed as the Son of God. All of these narratives were written 4,000 years before the birth of the Christian Son of God, "Jesus The Christ." Documentation for this can be found in the books of the ancient Egyptians, and inscribed on the walls of their temples.

It was at the Council of Nicea, in 332 A.D. that the emperor Constantine made Christianity the official state religion and abolished all competing religious ideology. At this conference, European images replaced the African images of the Madonna and Child.

Also at this conference, all original references to astrology and reincarnation were deleted from the European *Helios Biblos* and rewritten in allegorical form. This literary style of writing gives another meaning to each character, object and event to symbolically illustrate an idea, a moral or a religious principle.

In the sixth century A.D., the Emperor Justinian issued an edit abolishing the last vestiges of the African religious systems, and closed the last African Temple at Philae in Upper Egypt. At this temple, one can find inscriptions on the walls proclaiming the closing of the temple by Justinian, and the removal of scenes of the African Madonna and Child, Isis and Horus.

The Europeans then occupied numerous temples as their places of worship, etched crosses into the walls, and erected statues of the "new" Madonna and Child. Other historical escapades such as the Spanish Inquisition and the British Crusades, were attempts to impose this newly created religious ideology throughout the world.

These undeniable historical realities help to explain the existence of over 125 versions of the "Holy Bible." The word **version** is from the Latin word, *vertere* or *versum* which means to turn, to change or to translate.

Webster's dictionary defines the word **version** as meaning, *a change of form, a transformation, a conversion of a translation or rendering; an account or description from a particular point of view especially as contrasted with another account or point of view.* So many of our religious beliefs are influenced and determined by the particular version of the Bible we read.

One of the most common versions of the Bible is the *Authorized King James Version* which was first published in 1611. Its creation was necessitated, in 1534, after King Henry VIII and the Church of England separated from the Vatican. The closing years of the reign of King Henry VIII were characterized by restrictive measures regarding who could read and use the Bible.

As prohibited by an act of parliament, no woman, unless she were a woman of the noble class, was allowed to read the Bible. Also, no apprentices, journeymen, serving men or laborers were allowed to read or use any part of the Bible, without risking the pain of fines and imprisonment.

In 1604, King James authorized a committee of more than 50 learned men and scholars, to write one uniform translation of the Bible. By royal authority, the whole Church of England would be bound to this new Bible and no other versions could be read.

Clearly, it was during the writing of this particular version of the Bible, that old English pronouns and verbs such as "Ye," "Thee," "Thou," "Shalt" and other such terms were written into "The Good Book." Among the English scholars assigned to this committee was the great literary giant of that time, none other than William Shakespeare.

Shakespeare was forbidden by King James to publicize his involvement with the writing project, but the writer found a way to cleverly hide his "signature" within the material he wrote. Evidence of this can be found in the book of Psalms 46:3 and 46:9.

At the time of the writing of this version of the Bible, William Shakespeare was 46 years old. If you look at Psalm 46, you will note that the 46th word from the beginning of the psalm is *"shake,"* and the 46th word from the end of the psalm is *"spear."* This clearly establishes Shakespeare's role in the writing of this important piece of literature.

One reality that must be faced is that no matter what version of the Bible you presently read, the stories in the Bible are stories about African people. Over 70 references to Egypt and Ethiopia are mentioned in the Bible, more than any other nation. Much of what was written about Christianity originated in Africa because Europe, as we know it now, did not exist during that time.

The story of Jesus Christ is the story of conflict and rebellion against the invading forces of the Roman armies. At that time, Rome was the most powerful military force in the world. This story is the history of the oppression against people of color.

With this thought in mind, it seems strange that the oppressors of a religious movement would kill the Christian leader, and embrace the Christian religion in concept. Later they would designate themselves as the custodians of that religion and then move the religious faith to their homeland.

This would be the same as, stretching your mind to imagine, the South African government proclaiming Nelson Mandela as a national hero, and then erecting a shrine in his honor in Pretoria. Anytime a ruling class embraces its enemy as the religious leader, it's probably due to a change of political strategy as opposed to a change of heart.

When the invading army moved the newly formed Christian religion from Africa to Rome, other changes took place. Probably the most significant of these changes was the use of different physical features in representations of the images of Jesus.

In 1508 the famous artist and painter, Michelangelo was commissioned to paint the ceiling of the Sistine Chapel in Rome. His relatives were used as models. For example, his aunt and uncle posed for renderings of the images of Adam and Eve, who we all know were born in Africa, and his cousin was the model for the painting of Jesus. Therefore, the image that many people now accept as the portrait of Jesus The Christ is a totally inaccurate one.

Many religious leaders acknowledge the biblical references to Jesus which describe him as having hair like lamb's wool and feet like burnt brass. Even to this day, Europeans in Poland, Russia, Germany and Italy still worship at the Shrine of the Black Madonna and

Child. Even in churches where the statues are no longer visible, the black figures have not been destroyed, but are stored away in hidden places in the church where they are worshipped by a select few.

The story of the Immaculate Conception and the story of the Virgin Birth are stories which originated over 4,000 years ago in Ancient Nubia (Egypt). Osiris, Horus and Isis were prototypes for the contemporary versions of the Father, Son and Holy Ghost. Unfortunately, Christianity has limited the significance of the female and reduced her role to the vague and nebulous position of a Holy Ghost.

Much of the Bible is written in allegorical form. These writings are stories in which people, places and things symbolically represent higher moral truths which were known only to a select group of men.

The word "Christ" is a title, not a name, just as the word President is a title or King is a title. The word **Christ** means *the anointed one* or *one whose head is anointed with oil.* **Bethlehem** means *brain* or *house of God.* And the word **Jerusalem** means *heart. So what do they mean when they speak of Christ coming down from Bethlehem into Jerusalem?*

Christ becomes the Anointed One when oil is secreted from the brain, through the circulatory system, into the heart and is distributed throughout the entire body. So the allegory of this event involving Christ, Bethlehem and Jerusalem, symbolizes a transformative process which takes place within the human body.

In ancient African religion, the heart was viewed as the seat of the soul. This is important. The "Anointed One" refers to any person who has manifested within their bodies, special talents and abilities. Throughout the ages, many persons have been given the title "Christ," the existence of at least 16 has been documented.

The first Christ in recorded history was an African named Imhotep, who lived around the time 2980 B.C. Imhotep is the first recorded multi-genius in the history of mankind. He was a doctor, lawyer, grand vizier (prime minister) for the King Zoser. He was also the architect of the step pyramid.

Imhotep was a poet, the man responsible for giving us the phrase, "Eat, Drink And Be Merry, For Tomorrow You Will Die." He was the first Christ in recorded history and he lived almost 3,000 years before the birth of Jesus, the "Anointed One."

The date of the birth of Jesus has long been regarded as a day of deep religious significance. Allegorically, it speaks to the birth of this transforming process within the mind and body of man. The birthday of the Sun-God (Son-God) was also celebrated 4,000 years ago in the Egyptian temple of Abydos on the 25th of December.

From December 21st (the winter solstice) to December 24, the length of the days is approximately the same. On December 25 the Sun is symbolically born as sunlight increases approximately one minute per day. At the midnight hour during the first minute of December 25, the birth of the "sun" was seen in the astrological sign of Capricorn, which was known as the Stable of Augeus. Therefore, the infant Sun-God (Son-God), or the "New Sun," was said to have been "born in a stable."

Shining brightly on the meridian was Sirius, the Star from the East, while rising in the east was Virgo, the Virgin, with the horizon line passing through her center. From the positioning of this star developed the story of the famous star in the East which led the three Kings to worship the newly born Son-God who was born in the stable.

At the winter solstice, the sun is at its southern most position in the celestial sphere. After that date, it begins to travel northward along the ecliptic and at the vernal equinox (Spring), it "passes over" the celestial equator. This passing over of the sun from the south to the north of the equator was the origin of the Easter festival for the Passover.

References to astrology in the Bible can be found by understanding the movable feast called Easter, which is the first Sunday after the first full moon following the spring equinox. After the equinox, the "Sun" is resurrected and the number of daylight hours increases steadily until the summer solstice.

The resurrection of the "Sun" activates the life giving properties within all vegetation and restores life to the planet. In ancient Egypt,

Osiris was viewed as the first symbol of a resurrected savior, and his image was often painted green to represent the growth of vegetation.

When the sun reached the equinotical point and crossed over or passed over the equator 3,000 years ago, it was situated in the astrological sign of Aries, the Ram or the Lamb. Thus the symbol of the Passover Lamb representing God, gives a clue to the origin of the Passover Lamb as a type of crucified Christ. When Christ was born 2,000 years ago, the sun was in the astrological sign of Pisces the Fish. Thus Jesus is symbolically presented as the Fisherman of Men.

The African influences on European religion are numerous. An early temple of the Goddess Isis (Para Isidos) erected in France, is the origin of the word Paris. It is at the site of this former temple that we now find the Cathedral of Notre Dame, and the Grande Dame that was referred to is none other than Isis.

At the Vatican in Rome, we find an African obelisk in the center of St. Peter's square. The Pope's crown and staff are patterned after the crown and staff of the Pharaoh of Upper Egypt, who was regarded as God's representative on earth and The Good Shepherd. The cross, symbol of the death and crucifixion of Christ, is quite similar to the Egyptian Ankh, the symbol of life.

It is interesting to note how people of other nations responded to the imposition of certain religious doctrines on their culture and society. The Protestant Church evolved out of the struggle of people who "protested" against the religious beliefs that were imposed upon them. What began as a political, revolutionary and spiritual movement almost 2,000 years ago, has been grossly misrepresented and over commercialized to manipulate the minds and pocketbooks of the masses.

I'm very concerned about the commercialization of Christian holidays. Other major religious organizations strictly forbid the exploitation of their sacred rituals and their divine doctrines. Western religions seem to thrive on commercialization and exploitation of their deity.

The creation of Thanksgiving as a national holiday was lobbied by merchants who wanted to stimulate spending during the weeks prior to Christmas. The day for highest retail sales is the day after Thanksgiving, which also marks the official beginning of the Christmas season.

In 1938 President Franklin Roosevelt shifted Thanksgiving Day From November 30 to November 23, to give retailers a longer Christmas shopping season. Roosevelt's actions created a storm of protest that caused many citizens to refer to November 30 as the "Republican Thanksgiving Day", and November 23 as the "Democratic Thanksgiving Day".

Department store merchants became increasingly wealthy as many "pre-programmed" consumers spent a small fortune on gifts just to make their loved ones happy. The irony of this shopping madness can be witnessed the day after Christmas when sales reduce prices for all merchandise purchased at higher rates before Christmas.

A similar shopping phenomenon can be witnessed in the days leading up to Easter. Everyone must make certain that they're dressed to kill in their new shoes, new dresses, new suits and new hats, all to be worn to Church for Easter Sunday service.

I don't mean to sound like a spoilsport, but it seems to me that the religious significance of both Christmas and Easter are overshadowed by emotions of materialism. These same emotions are passed on to our children through the fabrication of such fictitious individuals as Santa Claus

Malcolm Aaron

and the Easter Bunny. This lays the emotional foundation for another generation of "pre-programmed" consumers. But this is not the first time that religion was used to make a fortune at the expense of other people.

The history of Christianity should be of particular note to African Americans because of its key role in the development of the slave trade. In 1411 A.D., Portuguese slave traders presented the first slaves to the Pope, who deemed these Africans to be soulless individuals. Is it a coincidence that the same mentality that created organized crime, the Mafia, also created organized religion and sanctioned the beginning of the slave trade?

The first ship to transport slaves from Africa to America was named "The Jesus." Slave masters used religion to control their slaves, promising eternal salvation in exchange for strict adherence to the laws of GOD. Slavery was sanctioned by the church through "Divine Providence" as a means of bringing salvation to a "soulless people."

The influence of religion on African Americans has been extensive. From Malcolm to Martin, from Powell to Young, from Jackson to Farrakhan, many of our political and civil rights leaders have come from religious backgrounds. As we approach the 21st Century, we are at a point in our lives where we must consider both new spiritual leadership and a new political direction. In reality, one fact stands out clearly for African Americans -- there is no separation between Church and State.

The term **RELIGION** comes from the words **RE** which means *back* and **LIGON** which means *to hold* or *to bind*. So the process of religion is the process of binding back to the source of your creation. Religion should provide correct rules of daily living that will help you to understand, strengthen and maintain your association with your Creator and your fellow man.

Ironically, the African concepts of spiritual liberation were distorted and used to impose physical and mental bondage. Originally, religion was viewed as the path to salvation, it later became the deification of man and was used to enslave and manipulate. We must all be aware of the strong influence that religious doctrines, principles and symbols have on all aspects of our lives.

Just consider this information. Think about it. Read additional resource materials. Do your own research and then . . . DON'T BE AFRAID TO DECIDE FOR YOURSELF.

References

ben-Jochannan, Yosef, *Chronology of the Bible*, New York, NY, Alkebu-lan Books Associates, 1972.

ben-Jochannan, Yosef, *black Man of the Nile*, New York, NY, Alkebu-lan Books Associates, 1981.

Jackson, John G., *Christianity Before Christ*, New York, NY, The Blyden Society, 1938.

Jackson, John G., *Man, God and Civilization*, Secaucus, NJ, Citadel Press, 1972.

Graves, Kersey, *Sixteen Crucified Saviors*, New York, NY, The Truth Seeker Company, 1960.

Drake, St. Clair, *The Redemption of Africa and Black Religion*, Chicago, IL, Third World Press, 1970.

Campbell, Joseph, *The Power of Myths*, New York, NY, Doubleday, 1988.

Mosley, William, *What Color Was Jesus*, Chicago, IL, African American Images, 1987.

A Brief History of Astrology
and the United States

The record shows that many of former President Ronald Reagan's activities such as his election campaigns, his presidential swearing-in ceremonies, his press conferences, medical care services and other events of earthly importance were all decided using the guidance of the stars and other heavenly bodies. Don Regan's book *For The Record* has revealed that Nancy Reagan often consulted an astrologist. But presidential aides have tried to decrease any attention given to the subject in an effort to end the inquiries from the media about the use of astrology in the White House.

For those who know and understand the science of *star logic*, better known as astrology, one question comes to mind, "Why didn't the knowledge of astrology and its role in politics come to light before now?" In actuality, astrology has been a major part of politics for thousands of years, not only in this country, but worldwide.

When you dig deeper, you'll find that astrology has played a major role in politics and has also been a key factor in making important political decisions. Reagan is surely not the first president to consult the stars. The very foundation of this country is rooted in the principals of astrology and numerology.

The "Founding Fathers" not only practiced the "occult arts" but also planned specific dates to coincide with celestial events. The birthday of the United States, July 4, 1776, was timed to coincide with the astrological sign of Cancer and the number 13.

Africa is ruled by the sun sign Cancer. The U.S. was founded on African principals and built by African slaves. July 4 follows 13 days after the sun entered the sign of Cancer during the summer solstice on June 21 in 1776.

Thirteen is a number which has profound numerological significance. There were 13 original colonies, the number 13 is repeated 13 times on the Great Seal of the United States and the 13th amendment to the constitution freed the slaves. All of these references to the number 13, and numerous others, are surely no coincidence.

For years the number 13 has come to represent powers of transformation and rebirth. Twelve has come to symbolize the completion

of a cycle and thirteen represents the energy of that cycle transcending itself into a higher, often spiritual, plane of existence.

We see this pattern repeated in the stories of Christ with his twelve apostles. King Arthur had twelve knights at his round table. The sun exists along with the twelve signs of the zodiac. Courtroom proceedings include the judge and the twelve men of the jury.

It is also no coincidence that presidential elections are held the first Tuesday, following the Monday, of the eleventh month of every leap year. Elections take place at this time because of the significance of the leap year (366 days) and the numerological significance of Tuesday's and the month of November.

Astrologically speaking, each day of the week is governed by a celestial body. Sunday is ruled by the Sun, Monday is ruled by the Moon, Tuesday is ruled by Mars and the pattern continues for the rest of the week, the month and the year.

Mars is regarded as the Roman god of war, whose astrological symbol is identical to the medical symbol for man. Wars have traditionally been fought and declared by men who were often voted into office. Since the right to vote had historically been restricted to men, it was only fitting that elections were held on a day associated with men -- Tuesday. The practice continues to this day.

To the layperson, all this talk about stars and numbers might be a bit confusing. That is by design. Knowledge which has the power to liberate the mind is usually limited to a select few, or this knowledge is criticized so that it becomes undesirable for the masses of people.

In the meantime, those in power or those who desire more power (almost always men), keep metaphysical consultants close at hand.

Some of the greatest rulers, in both ancient and modern times, relied on knowledge of the stars to guide their actions. This is science fact . . . not science fiction.

Adolph Hitler used astrologers and other occult practitioners before he used his armies. The swastika is a symbol which has been in use for thousands of years. When facing one direction it symbolizes creation, when reversed (as Hitler used it) it symbolizes destruction.

During World War II, Winston Churchill consulted astrologers in an attempt to know what Hitler was planning. It is a documented fact that the U.S., in conjunction with British intelligence, employed psychics. Each attempted to project his consciousness into the war rooms of Hitler's generals.

To this very day, both the Department of the Navy and the Soviet military are experimenting with methods of "psychic warfare." Yet, we are told that psychic phenomenon, astrology and numerology are all pseudo sciences which lack any scientific foundation.

Astrology is one of the oldest sciences known to mankind. Everyone should be aware of the fact that the sun and the moon have a profound affect on the earth. High tides, high crime rates, births and deaths all follow cycles related to the stars and other heavenly bodies.

Over 500 years ago, scientists believed that the earth was flat and that it was the center of the universe. New scientific discoveries are made almost every day, indicating that scientists are still learning about the earth and our solar system.

Just because scientists and politicians don't sanction astrology and related disciplines doesn't mean that these studies lack merit. Oftentimes, many things that are not properly understood are labeled bogus by the status quo. As Stevie Wonder said, "When you believe in things you don't understand, you suffer."

In any event, time will tell . . . it usually does.

References

Churchward, Albert, *Origin and Evolution of Freemasonry*, London, G. Allen & Unwin, 1920.

Hall, Manley P., *Secret Teachings of All Ages*, Los Angeles, CA, Philosophical Research Society, 1978.

Tompkins, Peter, *The Magic of Obelisks*, New York, NY, Harper & Row, 1981.

Signs of the Times

When you hear the robins singing happily in the trees, you consider this a sure sign of the approaching spring season and the return of warm weather. What if you see a suspicious looking person standing in an alley? Perhaps you might view his presence as a sign of danger, and a good reason to be on guard in order to avoid any trouble.

Signs are wonderful things. They tell us where we are, where we are going, or where we have been. When we properly interpret signs, they can yield some valuable information.

If you want to understand signs and the events they are announcing, learn how to interpret them. Every coming event is preceded by specific tell-tale signs. To be forewarned is to be forearmed, and hindsight is 20/20 vision. In order for you to read and understand the signs of current events, you will need to develop a special kind of vision called *insight*.

The frequent incidents of child abuse, murders and teenage suicides are all signs that this nation is in deep trouble. Every day we are shocked with new revelations of madness and cold-blooded brutality. People are asking themselves how and why this is happening. Is this a sign from God or what?

What is happening, in no uncertain terms, is the law of **KARMA** in operation. Karma is the universal law of reciprocity – better known as *cause and effect*. After the assassination of President John Kennedy, Malcolm X referred to this phenomenon as *"America's chickens coming home to roost."* In more familiar terms, he was describing *"What goes around, comes around."*

Applying this philosophy to history yields some interesting perspectives. Each chapter in the story of mankind was preceded by signs which indicated the direction that particular societies would take in their growth and development. It is quite easy to look back at a series of historical events and determine what led to certain inevitable conclusions.

America is a nation deeply rooted in violence. This country holds the distinction of being the wealthiest nation on the planet, but it is also the most violent nation. There are more people murdered in the United States in one month than are killed during an entire year in most countries.

Because of greed, there are people in America who have committed murder and promoted the use of bloodshed for so long that for them these acts have become second nature. For some people, a human life is seen as no more significant than the life of an insect.

The cruel and merciless disrespect of human life was the foundation upon which this nation was built. The destruction of the Red Man was followed by the destruction of the Black Man. Current signs of the times indicate that the European has turned on himself. Now they appear to be on a KARMIC collision course toward self-destruction, and the madness shows no sign of ending.

Any time the value systems of a society tolerate pre-teen and teenage sexploitation, that society should not be surprised when these problems manifest themselves on a larger scale. Social groups have to be morally bankrupt to tolerate the sexploitation of children. In American society, child molesters are rarely criminally punished. All to often, they're simply slapped on the wrists and released back into society. This is tantamount to giving a seal of approval to this madness and does little to discourage potential victimizers.

The youth of America see the hypocrisy and disrespect for human life that this country displays. Many of them choose not to be a part of the confusion and sometimes adopt antisocial behavior patterns. Sure, there are a number of available options, but not for those unable to clearly see possible alternatives. Fear seems to present only one tragic choice – self-destruction. Many young people decide that suicide is one way to escape.

America is a nation in big trouble. One does not have to be a prophet to see the handwriting on the wall and read the signs of the time.

The key to surviving this national insanity is to learn how to live in the world, and not of it. Cause and effect works both ways. You can create the causes that produce the desirable effects.

If you wish to produce positive effects you must first generate positive causes. You get out of life what you put into it.

The time for apathy and inactivity is long gone. You cannot idly sit around complaining and waiting for things to change. Either you make things happen, or things happen to you. Believe that you count and that you can make a difference. The signs of the times will reflect your new belief.

References

Brown, Dee, *Bury My Heart at Wounded Knee*, New York, NY, Washington Square Press, 1984.

Hill, Robert B., *The Strengths of the Black Family*, New York, NY, Emerson Hall, 1972.

Eat, Drink and Be Merry . . .

Diet and African Americans

Ham, potato salad, french fries, pork chops, ice cream, egg nog, chitterlings, t-bone steak, cakes, pies, cookies, cornbread, macaroni and cheese, wine, liquor and beer – face it, black folks buy and consume a lot of food and drink during the Thanksgiving, Christmas and New Years holiday season. Though you eat, drink and make merry, wishing the good cheer of a long life, peace and prosperity, the food choices that you make may end your life prematurely. Without a doubt, by eating foods fried in heavy grease and with excessive concentrations of sugar and salt, you may be feasting your way to an early grave.

We've definitely allowed a killer to run loose in the black community. This killer is responsible for more deaths than drugs or black-on-black crime. This killer makes all age groups its victims, stalking its prey during all hours of the day and night. This killer is responsible for the high infant mortality rate and the slow, miserable death of many of our senior citizens. This killer is the diet of the African American people.

The Washington, D.C. community was shocked several years ago when an ad campaign sponsored by the American Cancer Society stated: *"If you are black and live in D.C. you stand a greater chance of dying of cancer.* Many thought the ads were racist in their approach, but they were frank and to the point, and they told the truth, whether we wanted to hear it or not.

Cancer of the colon is the most common form of cancer in blacks. Colon cancer is as intricately related to diet as alcoholism is related to drinking or lung cancer to smoking. The colon is an essential part of the digestive system. If we are dying because our food is not being properly digested, then we must reconsider the foods that we put into our bodies.

The body is basically designed to heal itself. It has the capacity to regenerate over two billion new cells every day. The energy necessary to maintain this process is derived from the foods that we eat. If your diet is not providing you with the proper nutrients, your body cannot do its job. We will get sick and continue to get sick until we either change our diets or die. These are the only two choices that we have.

Many people don't know it, but the worst possible food you can put into your body is meat. The human digestive tract is not designed to process meat. Any food which stays in your body for more than eight hours is going to cause problems. It takes meat an average of 90 hours to be digested. During that time, undigested pieces of meat will remain in the colon and rot, sending toxins into the body which slowly kill you.

The soul food that we so proudly claim is our worst enemy. This food causes bloated stomachs, varicose veins, swollen ankles, high blood pressure, heart disease and a number of other related illnesses. I am sure that everyone knows at least 10 black people who have suffered or died from high blood pressure, diabetes or heart disease. The sad truth of the matter is that these illnesses can be significantly reduced by changing our diets.

Without your health, you have nothing. Money, power or friends can do little to correct the harm which we bring upon ourselves by eating improper foods. Since the purpose of this essay is to inform and enlighten the reader, I would fail to accomplish my purpose if I did not include some helpful guidelines for improving the quality of your health. Please practice the following positive health tips:

1. Stay interested in your health and nutrition.

2. Cut down on food intake.

3. Remove foods high in sugar content (candies, cakes, pies, rolls, ice cream and refined sugar).

4. Replace junk foods with fruits, fruit juices and nuts.

5. Replace dairy products such as milk and eggs with their organic counterparts. Organic foods are those produced by nature such as fresh fruits and vegetables.

6. Replace meats with organic chicken and fish.

7. Completely remove all inorganic foods from your diet; that is, all synthetic, highly processed, man-made foods.

8. Work toward being a healthy and vigorous individual.

9. Fast one day a week.

10. Drink 2 glasses of water (room temperature) upon rising each morning.

11. Water helps eliminate toxins in the body, and flushes the body to help prevent colds and flu.

12. If you are sick, sufficient amounts of water can reduce the complications of fever.

13. Water is the oldest, safest diuretic known. Monitoring your urine will tell you about the quantity of water in the body. Your urine should be clear and not yellow.

14. Body poisons are released through the kidneys – sufficient water reduces the risk of infection because of an overconcentration of urine.

15. Fluid is much more important to human life than food. A person fasting can live two months on water alone. Without water he or she could only live two weeks.

I believe in drawing on my life experiences and the experiences of those around me, which is why I adopted a vegetarian lifestyle many years ago. Believe me when I tell you that it does make a difference. Granted, it's not for everyone, but if you can regulate your diet you can regulate your health. You are what you eat. Think about this when you sit down to your next meal at the dinner table.

References

Muhammed, Elijah, *How to Eat to Live*, Chicago, IL, Muhammed Mosque of Islam #2, 1967.

Gregory, Dick, *Cooking With Mother Nature*, New York, NY, Harper & Row, 1971.

Kloss, Jethro, *Back to Eden*, Ashland, OR, World Wide OR, 1984.

Kushi, Machio, *The Book of Microbiotics*, Japan, Japan Publishing, 1977.

Sports and African Americans

There was a tremendous response from all segments of society regarding the comments made by Jimmy "the Greek" Snyder, just prior to the 1988 Superbowl. CBS repudiated him, others called his remarks racist, while some said that he was historically correct.

The noteworthiness of the entire affair is that all three viewpoints are right. From my perspective the comments made by "The Greek" were as simple as ABC.

A. *"The black is the better athlete."*

B. *"The only thing that the whites control is the coaching jobs."*

C. *"The black is a better athlete because he's been bred to be that way."*

Jimmy "The Greek" was only expressing the beliefs widely held by his associates--network executives, team owners, coaches and gamblers. CBS had no choice but to fire "The Greek" because he exposed the inner feelings of an elite group of men.

Snyder's comments concerning the selective breeding of blacks are historically accurate. African Americans are the only race of people on this planet who were enslaved and systematically bred like cattle for over 400 years. The fact stands as an undeniable blight on the face of this country.

Upon further scrutiny, "The Greek's" remarks revealed a racist mindset with a myopic view of history. To say that "the black" is better just because of selective breeding denies the long and rich heritage of black people. This is truly *"his-story"* in its most racist form, making others believe that whites made an already "great people" greater.

Blacks are locked out of coaching and managerial positions because of inequities built into the system. On the playing field this is called cheating. Racism (cheating) is the only way that an inherently inferior group can consistently beat a genetically superior group on or off the playing field.

Whenever the roadblocks of racism were removed, blacks usually excelled. It was once widely believed by whites that blacks could only catch a football, but not throw one, because our bodies were made strictly for running and jumping. During Superbowl XXII, however, not only did the first black quarterback lead his team to vic-

tory . . . but he also shattered all previous quarterbacking records in the process.

What is conveniently overlooked in the breeding issue is that it takes brain tissue to control muscle tissue. Acute muscle response – superior jumping, running and throwing – are directly associated with superior mental faculties. The ability to process enormous bits of information in microseconds is one of the many attributes of persons with high concentrations of melanin in their bodies. *(More interesting facts on the qualities of melanin can be read in the essay entitled, The Mysteries of Melanin.)*

A mind that can allow you to jump high can also think high. This is the genetic legacy of the African. An unbiased view of history shows the glorious accomplishments of African people dating back thousands of years. In January 1988, Newsweek magazine revealed to the world that the parents of all humanity were an African couple affectionately called *Adam and Eve.*

Newsweek said blacks were the first people, and Jimmy "The Greek" revealed to America what whites have done to manipulate us. This is truly an interesting chapter in African American history. *(See essay entitled, The Mother of Mankind.)*

There are some who wish to separate black history from African history, which is like separating a child from its mother and denying their relationship. To separate the African-American child from its African mother is to deny that child its cultural and spiritual nourishment.

Snyder calls himself "The Greek" because he is culturally nourished by the spirit of his ancestry. His version of history places the Greeks at the forefront of culture and civilization. Snyder wears his ethnicity as a badge for all to see. Thanks to the research of many Afrocentric historians, however, we now know that the Greek origin of civilization is nothing more than a gross fabrication of human history.

Today, many football and basketball empires stand tall on a foundation built by black athletes. Jimmy "The Greek" was kicked out of the penthouse suite for inadvertently giving away the blueprints. Jimmy got exactly what he deserved for residing in such a racist institution.

Ultimately, I feel that Snyder's remarks will lead to the renovation of these "ivory towers." I can't think of a more fitting day for all of this controversy to have occurred than on the birthday of Dr. Martin Luther King.

References

Rogers, J.A., *From Superman to Man.* St. Petersburg, FL, Helga M. Rogers, 1968.

Rogers, J.A., *As Nature Leads*, Chicago, IL, M.A. Donohue, 1919.

Rogers, J.A. *Sex and Race* (Volumes I - III), St. Petersburg, FL, Helga Rogers, vol 1, 1967, vol 2, 1970, vol 3, 1944).

The Politics of Hair

All of your actions make a political statement, whether you're aware of it or not. A political statement can be a statement of policy made by an individual or a group. The type of foods you eat makes a political statement. The type of clothing you wear makes a political statement. Even the style you've chosen for wearing your hair makes a political statement. An excellent example of the politics of hair is demonstrated by the boycott of Revlon products led by black hair-care product manufacturers.

Historically, the politics of hair was closely correlated with the struggle for civil rights in America. In the 1930's and 1940's the desire of many *negroes* was to be integrated into the American mainstream. This was reflected in their desire to become white at the expense of their own blackness. Skin bleaching creams and process hairstyles were the order of the day. The closer these black men and women came to looking white, the better they felt about themselves.

With the advent of the civil rights movement in the 1950's, a different attitude prevailed. The desire to look white was replaced by a desire to be treated like a human being. As blacks identified more closely with their African heritage, this increased their desire to regain their natural look. A stronger identification with a homeland motivated blacks to stand up to racism and demand their fair share. Racial identification brought on racial pride and self respect.

This attitude became even more popular in the 1960's. The "power to the people movement" increased the desire among blacks to wear their hair in *natural* styles. Blacks sang and danced to the words of James Brown's song, *"How you gonna get respect if you ain't cut your process yet?"* Hair definitely made a political statement. Malcolm X even credited this train of thought with motivating the Hippie and Back to Nature Movements.

With political pressure brought to bear, civil rights legislation was passed opening doors which had previously been closed. The evidence speaks for itself. The more blacks respected themselves and respected their culture, the more they were respected by their oppressors.

With the advent of the 1970's, a new phenomenon evolved. Cries of *"power to the people"* were replaced by the selfish declaration of *"it's your thing, do what you want to do."* Many accomplishments gained

Malcolm Aaron

over a 15-year period were dissipated in a matter of years. The more complacent blacks became, the more ground they lost in the civil rights movement. Self-identification gave way to identification, once again, with the oppressor.

The Afro hairstyles of the 1960's disappeared and became the "Super Fly look" of the 1970's. Males, who had at one time demanded to be respected as men, were now wearing permanents, curlers in their hair, high-heeled shoes and handbags.

History clearly points out that as blacks lost their sense of political awareness, they also lost the respect of the European community. Laws that were passed to create equality of the races were now seen as generating an atmosphere of reverse discrimination. As blacks were lulled into a sense of false security and feeling that it was no longer necessary to proclaim a sense of cultural awareness, numerous gains were lost.

The current decade of the 1980's reflects a continued demise of civil rights gains. The resurgence of racism proves that this cancer of ignorance was only in remission in the body of America.

It is obvious that blacks have lost a considerable degree of political awareness. Jherri Curls, Finger Waves and "Do Rags" are the fashion of the day. Our lack of self-respect is directly proportional to the increase of racism and racial intolerance towards African

Americans. *"If you don't respect yourself, how in the world do you expect anybody to respect you?"*

Hair makes a political statement. One should not become a slave to fashion at the expense of his civil rights. Billions of dollars are spent annually on black hair care at a time when black colleges, businesses and organizations are facing financial ruin.

Yes, we all have an individual right to choose how we will wear our hair. However, we also have a collective responsibility not to sacrifice political gains for cosmetic appearances. Every act expresses a political statement.

First impressions are lasting. Impressions of self-awareness and self-pride evoke a corresponding response. Impressions of a faddish nature reflect someone who is not to be taken seriously and implies a level of political naiveté.

References

Haley, Alex, *The Autobiography of Malcolm X*, (pp 53-55), New York, NY, Grove Press, 1964.

Karenga, Maulana, *Introduction to Black Studies*, Los Angeles, CA, Kawaida Publications, 1982.

Asante, Molefi, *Afrocentricity*, Trenton, NJ, African World Press, 1988.

A Sense of Sight

If you were given a choice, would you rather lose your sense of taste, touch, smell, hearing or sight? Think about it! Of your five senses, your sense of sight is probably the most precious. Given the option, I'm sure the majority of you would sacrifice one of your other senses rather than your sense of sight.

If you were fortunate, you were born into this world with a pair of eyes that will serve you from the cradle to your grave. Interestingly enough, our eyes are the only part of our bodies that don't increase significantly in size from the time of birth. It's as if we are born with a full grown pair of eyes.

The human eye measures about one inch in diameter. Yet, it can see objects as far away as a star, and as tiny as a grain of sand. Actually, your eyes do not see objects. Instead, they process light waves that objects either absorb or reflect.

The eye can be conditioned to see in bright light and in very dim light. The Dogon people in West Africa can see stars with their naked eyes that are nearly impossible to see even with telescopes. Over the centuries, their eyes have been conditioned to focus and process light waves received from great distances.

The visual processing of communication messages through the eyes has always been of vital importance for human survival. However, the technological advances of today's society have added a new dimension to sight. There has been much discussion concerning black consumers and their decisions to wear colored contact lenses in their eyes. I am one of the many critics strongly against the wearing of colored contact lenses. Following are the reasons why.

The two most noticeable parts of the eye are the iris and pupil. The iris is the large, colored portion of the eye. Its color comes from a brownish-black substance called melanin. This substance is the same as the melanin which gives skin its color. The iris of the eye is just like the skin. Darker colored eyes have a greater melanin content.

In addition to giving the iris color, melanin absorbs excessive light that might otherwise dazzle and overwhelm the eyes, causing blurred vision. This is the very reason why football and baseball players put darkener under their eyes to absorb intense sunlight and maintain a clear line of vision.

At the center of the iris is a round opening called the pupil. The pupil regulates the amount of light that enters the eye. When the eyes are exposed to strong, bright light, the pupils become as small as pinheads to prevent eye damage. In the dark, or in dimly lit rooms, the pupils can become as large as the entire iris in order to let in as much light as possible and improve visibility.

When light enters the eye, it is changed into electrical signals which travel to the brain. The brain translates these signals into images which provide us with mental pictures of what we're seeing. All of this happens within fractions of a second. It's a definite fact that when the iris is dark in color, the transmission of light signals to the brain from the eye takes place much more efficiently.

So, why in the world would anyone want to make their dark eyes lighter? This is beyond reason. Unfortunately, we live in a world where European standards of beauty such as blue eyes and blond hair are imposed on the entire world population, the vast majority of which is non-European. When was the last time you saw someone with blue eyes wearing brown contact lenses?

Some blacks say that certain hairstyles, and colored contacts are only a fashion statement. They ignore the political and psychological implications of their acceptance of these fashions. If you saw a

European wearing an Afro or dreadlock hairstyle, you would be correct in assuming that he was trying to emulate African culture?

The same concept applies to African Americans who adopt non-Afrocentric mores. Wearing colored contacts in an attempt to blend into mainstream America can be detrimental to your health. Recent scientific research shows that lesser amounts of melanin in the eyes increases the risk for eye cataracts.

The marketing of colored lenses in the black community has been quite aggressive. The product's endorsement by celebrities only enhances the appeal in the minds of other impressionable people.

One optometrist recalls that when colored contacts were first introduced, blacks requested hazel-colored contacts, but were told that they were unavailable. Now that many people have purchased blue and green contacts, they suddenly find the introduction of hazel-colored lenses. What a great marketing strategy! Once again, the bottom line is money.

Everyone is certainly entitled to do whatever they wish with their body. We all are entitled to our right to be wrong. Our eyesight, however, is not something to be taken *LIGHTLY!*

References

Fanon, Franz, *Black Skin/White Mask*, New York, NY, Grove Press, 1967.

Akbar, Na'im, *Chains and Images of Psychological Slavery*, Jersey City, NJ, New Minds Production, 1984

Asante, Molefi, *Afro Centric Idea*, Philadelphia, PA, Temple University Press, 1987.

Griaule and Dieterlen, *The Pale Fox*, Chino Valley, AZ, Continuum Foundation, 1986.

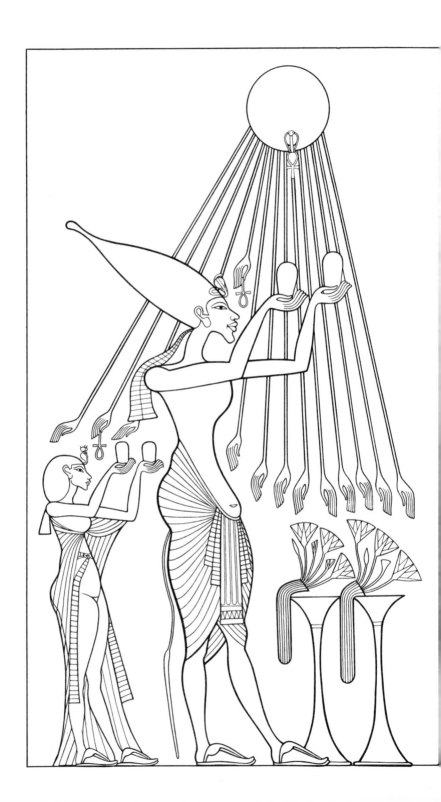

Paying Homage to the Sun

It is 93 million miles away, yet it exerts the most powerful force on the planet.

It is the radiant day star, which blazes down on us from the heavens, and is the giver of all life.

It has been the oldest and most common object of worship in the history of mankind.

It is the sun.

All living things hunger for the light and warmth of the sun that falls on us like a blanket of love. The first day of the week was named in honor of it. The second day of the week, Monday, means day of the moon, which is illuminated by the sun.

The lengthening of the days and nights during the course of the year are the hallmarks of our four seasons. The spring and fall equinoxes signal a time of equal day and night on the planet. The summer and winter solstices represent the longest and shortest day of the year, respectively.

For over 5,000 years, people have acknowledged the sun as a symbol of goodness, strength and spiritual rebirth, and rightfully so. The sun is the power behind the process of photosynthesis, the means by which plants grow. Animals feed on the energy-enriched plants, and man uses both plants and animals for food, shelter and clothing.

The sun evaporates water from rivers, lakes and oceans which forms clouds, and water falls from these clouds as rain or snow. Clouds are visible bodies of fine droplets of water or particles of ice dispersed in the atmosphere which change the temperature and air pressure, thus influencing the weather on the earth below. After each rainstorm or snowstorm, the sun shines brightly in the sky to repeat the cycle and draw the water back up into the clouds.

If the sun stopped shining, all life would soon perish. The air would freeze and the earth would become nothing more than an empty waste – ball of rock drifting endlessly through space.

Man's interest in the sun goes back to his earliest days of existence in Africa. Africans noticed that the sun was responsible for the recurring pattern of day and night. They became aware, also, that the apparent daily path of the sun is high across the sky during the warmest season, and low during the rainy season, and that the seasons repeat themselves in the same manner as does day and night.

The sun became the guide for agriculture, and was later recognized as the central figure in religious ceremonies and regarded as the symbol of God. The sun was considered benevolent – the giver of light and life, the provider of food, and the guardian of justice. One of the earliest manifestations of the sun as a god was the god Amon. We still acknowledge His presence when we end our prayers with "Amen."

The ancient Egyptians had many names for the sun. These names represented the various positions of the sun during the course of the day. RA or RE represented the rising sun. This was the origin of the word RAY, as in ray of sun. HORUS was the God representing the noon sun. And from Horus is derived the word *hour* which indicates the relative position of the sun to the earth at any given moment. SET represented the setting sun and the coming of darkness. The sun rises in the east and sets in the west, thus the familiar usage of the term *sunset*. AMON symbolized the hidden or unseen force of the sun after setting. As mentioned earlier, the word "AMEN," which is the well-known closing for many of our prayers, was taken from one of the earliest names for the SUN-GOD, AMON. We're all very familiar with, "*Now and Forever, Amen*," as well as, "*And Deliver us from Evil, Amen.*"

In June, we celebrate the summer solstice, which marks the longest day of the year and heralds the beginning of the summer. After June 25, the days begin to shorten as the sun appears to move backwards across the heavens. This backward movement was referred to astrologically as the sign Cancer, which, like the crab that it symbolizes, also moves backwards.

Between the summer solstice and winter solstice fall two equally important occasions, the spring and fall equinoxes. Solstice is a word which means *sun is still*, and equinox means *equal night*, which also implies an increase in the amount of light and power from the sun, and equal disbursement or reduction of this solar energy.

The ancient Egyptians' attraction to the sun was so strong that they often referred to themselves as "*Sons and Daughters of Light*," or "*Children of the Sun.*" When a person is exposed to sunlight, it produces an obvious change in skin complexion, but, when dark-skinned people are exposed to sunlight, it also produces a physiological change inside the body caused by the release of the hormone melatonin. Studies have proven that melatonin increases one's level of perception and spirituality.

The sun's energy is greatest during the times of the summer and winter solstices, and the spring and fall equinoxes. For this reason, certain Egyptian *holy days*, or *holidays* as they are now called, occurred during these times of year. For example, December 25th is the first day of increased daylight to follow the December 21st solstice. As discussed in the essay on *"Little Known Facts About Religion"* this Egyptian *holy day* was celebrated more than 4,000 years before the birth of the *son-god* Jesus the Christ. As a matter of fact, in those days the words *sun* and *son* were synonymous.

Even if we ignore the religious and symbolic significance of the sun, we still cannot deny its impact on our lives. We naturally respond favorably to the increased number of hours of daylight in the summer months, and brood over the absence of light and warmth during the winter.

The sun's energy is stored in coal and oil which is commonly used to operate the generators that provide our cities with light, heat and air conditioning. This is also the source for fuel which runs our vehicles. Coal and oil were produced many millions of years ago from the decaying remains of plants and animals whose bodies were once exposed to the life giving rays of the sun.

The earth has experienced approximately 5 billion years of sunrises and sunsets. Whether it falls on the flowers in the garden or on the sunbathers at the beach, the sun's energy has traveled 93 million miles in eight minutes and 20 seconds in order to reach the earth.

The radiant energy from the sun is so intense that the only thing that prevents this heat from roasting the flowers or baking the sunbathers is a thin protective layer, miles above the earth's surface, called *ozone*. A relatively high concentration of ozone absorbs solar ultraviolet radiation that cannot be screened out by other atmospheric components. Scientists have recently discovered that the protective concentration of the ozone layer has been negatively affected by man made chemicals. Harmful rays of the sun, which were once filtered out, are now bombarding the planet with increased doses of radiation through an opening in the ozone layer.

This radiation is particularly harmful to people who lack skin pigmentation or melanin. Some groups of people are now experiencing more cases of skin cancer and other skin-related illnesses. Herpes is one such illness which affects primarily Europeans. Recently, the American Cancer Society ran a series of ads targeted specifically towards whites, and warned them that *any* exposure to the sun can cause skin cancer. Their message against sunbathing was definite and to the point, *"If you fry now, you'll pay later!"*

Of all of our studies, history is most qualified to reward all research. History has shown us that for thousands of years, people of color have lived in harmony with the sun and worshipped it as the source of life. They were blessed by the sun with dark-colored skin, which was seen as a sign of their "special relationship" with the sun. This "special relationship" can only be of benefit when one understands it and lives in harmony with the principals which the sun manifests.

References

De Lubicz, R.A. Schwaller, *Sacred Science*, Rochester, VT, Inner Traditions, 1961.

Lemay, Lucy, *Egyptian Mysteries*, New York, NY, Crossroad, 1981.

West, John Anthony, *Serpent in the Sky*, San Diego, CA, Crown Press, 1987.

Discover magazine, (p. 24), July, 1988.

The Mysteries of Melanin

Ever wonder why a sliced apple, banana, pear, eggplant or cabbage turns brown when left exposed to the air? That's melanin! Ever wonder why an open wound or sore turns dark brown or black when the protective scab forms during the healing process? That again is melanin!

Most people probably believe that melanin is only the pigment that gives color to our skin, hair and eyes. But research now shows that melanin is also found in our hearts, livers, nerves, muscles, intestines and 12 locations in our brains. Derivatives of melanin can also be found in our blood, our hormones and our cerebral spinal fluid.

In short, our bodies contain melanin from head to toe, inside and outside. Melanin is the substance which is responsible for our very existence. It is a healer, an energy absorber, a drug and an organizer of major body functions. It is now universally accepted that melanin is a total system unto itself.

Without a doubt, melanin is viewed as the "giver of life." It is present in both the sperm and egg and it supervises the growth of the developing fetus. The brain and spinal cord of every person was formed from melaninated cells within the growing embryo.

During the 2nd Annual Conference of Melanin Researchers, April 15 to 17, 1988, a dozen African American scholars met in New York City to discuss the scientific, historical, psychological and physiological aspects of melanin. I feel compelled to share more of this interesting and fascinating information with you.

Melanin is derived from the Greek word *melanos*, which means *black*. Melanin is the most important, the most complex and the most perfect molecule in the human body.

Every person on earth has varying amounts of melanin in his body. The key is, some people have more than others. In the bodies of Africans and African Americans, melanin is found in more sites and in greater concentrations than in any other race of people on earth.

The first people to inhabit the earth were Africans with blue-black skin, who lived on the equator. These Africans had high concentrations of melanin in their skin, which served to screen out the harmful ultraviolet light from the sun. In the African brain, a

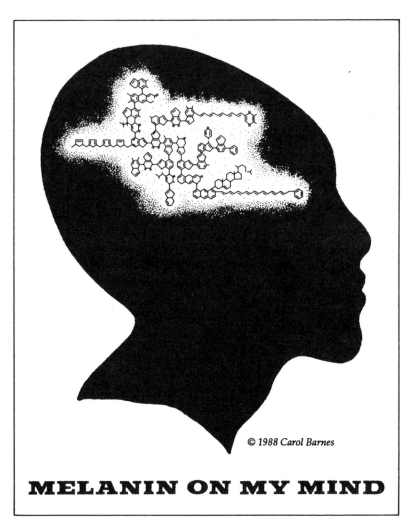

© 1988 Carol Barnes

MELANIN ON MY MIND

melanin hormone is secreted which is the essence of what we now call *soul*.

The more melanin there is in the skin, the darker it is and the less it ages from sunlight exposure. Scientifically speaking, black skin is 100 percent more efficient in screening out harmful ultraviolet light than white skin.

It is because of a lack of melanin, and the deterioration of the ozone, that whites are now warned to avoid exposure to sunlight. It has also been shown that both herpes and the AIDS virus are activated by ultraviolet light.

Think about it; the sun is the life giver, but for people who lack melanin, the sun means death. This black, light-absorbing molecule called melanin is recognized as one of the primary keys of life. Melanin is what makes people human. Melanin connects people to the creative forces of the universe.

Melanin has been found in the oceans, the soil and our food, particularly bananas, eggplants and greens. Melanin is present in clouds and stars, and it has even been discovered on the outer surface of Haley's comet. Melanin has been found to be active in unearthed bones which were over a million years old.

As ever present as melanin is, it still remains a mystery to scientists. It cannot be analyzed. It cannot be broken apart. It cannot be fingerprinted.

Melanin is influenced by the electro-magnetic field of the earth, by light waves and sound vibrations. Because of its magnetic properties, people with higher concentrations of melanin in their bodies are more in tune with nature.

We witness the power of melanin whenever we see African Americans performing on the football field, basketball court, at city hall, on television or in the theater. It's been said that blacks have to be twice as good as whites in order to compete with them. For blacks, melanin is the equalizer.

Melanin has been found to be a primary component in the creation and maintenance of the human race. In addition to the numerous physiological influences melanin has on the body, research now shows a definite relationship between melanin and spiritual awareness.

Historians Chancellor Williams and John Henrik Clarke have both stated that the African had a belief in the universality of God in all people. This allowed them to embrace the European as their brother, and grant him access to African soil, thereby setting up the conditions for the "Destruction of Black Civilizations."

Africans today are still suffering from this fatal error in judgment. However, two serious questions must be asked. "Why did the African see the European as a child of God,?" and, "Why did the European see the African as a soulless savage?"

The answers can be found in an examination of the differences between these two races of people and the presence, in the Africans,

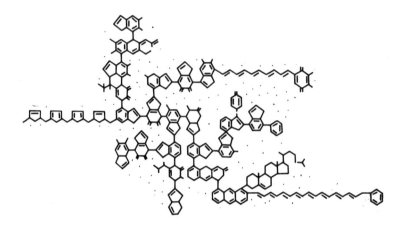

of a melanin derived chemical substance called melatonin. Melatonin can be described as a mentally or morally stimulating hormone produced by the pineal gland. It allows an individual to experience higher levels of spiritual awareness.

Scientific research has shown that some 85 percent of people with high concentrations of melanin in their skin (i.e., Africans, Hispanics, Indians and other "people of color") produce melatonin, while only 15 percent of people lacking melanin (principally Europeans) cannot produce this spiritually inducing substance. The reason for this dramatic difference in melatonin production is that the pineal gland (which regulates the activities of other glands in the body) is found to be calcified and nonfunctioning in people lacking substantial amounts of melanin. Could this be the reason why African Americans refer to each other as *soul brother* and *soul sister*, eat *soul food* and listen to *soul music*? Soul certainly has a spiritual connotation.

Historically, most people of color possess this quality called soul. Most have developed a system of salvation (religion) which is based on ancestral worship. The essence of ancestral worship is *necromancy*, or communication with the dead.

How does one communicate with the dead? It occurs naturally when you sleep. Every person alive has had a dream, at some time or another, in which they've spoken with a deceased relative or friend who offered them guidance or direction on problems they were facing.

How is it possible to see in your dreams? How is it possible to see with your two eyes closed? It is possible because when you sleep you see with your "inner eye." In some traditions this "inner eye" is called the "third eye," the eye of clairvoyance. Other traditions refer to this eye as the pineal gland.

It is when you are asleep that the pineal gland secretes the hormone melatonin (primarily during the hours of 2 a.m. to 6 a.m.) which literally bathes the brain, thus creating the chemical condition necessary for "inner vision" to take place.

The relationship between melatonin and spirituality is certainly nothing new. The revelations of the Bible, Torah, Koran and of the Buddha were all inspired by melanin-induced visions of people of color.

We cannot expect nonmelaninated people to explain to us, or even understand something which they themselves do not possess. This is all the more reason why the annual melanin conferences are of the utmost importance to people of color.

As our knowledge of melanin increases we will gain more insight into ourselves, both spiritually and physically. But the key is that the knowledge must come from us. We must develop the scientists, sociologists, and institutions necessary to carry out the research to expand our understanding of melanin . . . the key to life.

References

Welsing, Frances Cress, *Cress Theory of Color Confrontation*, Washington, D.C., C-R Publishers, 1970.

King, Dr. Richard, *Ureaus, The Journal of Unconscious Life*, (see article *Black Dot The Black Seed of Humanity*), Winter Solstice Issue, (vol 2, no. 1), Los Angeles, CA, Aquarian Spiritual Center, 1986.

Barnes, Carol, *Melanin: The Chemical Key to Black Greatness*, Houston, TX, Black Greatness Series, 1988.

The Wall Street Journal, August 26, 1988 (*Natural Tan* article).

Additional References

The KM-WR Science Consortium is an organization of African scholars who have begun to, from a multidisciplinary perspective, expand the dimension of analysis on melanin. Annual Melanin conferences are held to provide a forum for a greater understanding of the physical and psychological function of melanin. For additional information on upcoming conferences and publications, cassette and video tapes of previous conferences, contact:

KM-WR Science Consortium
P.O. Box 5704
Oakland, California 94605
(415) 638-4202

"We are living through a struggle of two forces on this earth, beasts who walk upside down and angels who walk right side up. The beasts that walk upside down in the world, control information and have distorted history. They try to get us to see the world through their distorted ideas and concepts. The beasts walk in darkness and are unable to tune into the light.

If you are walking upside down in darkness, tune into the light, read *From the Browder File*. The information presented in Tony Browder's book will help you to walk right side up."

Dr. Richard King M.D., Psychiatrist
Ass't Prof. of Black Studies, San Francisco State University
Founder of the Annual Conference of Melanin Scholars and Researchers,
San Francisco, CA

Afterword

Persons whose minds are hopeful, confident, courageous, persistent, and determined on a set purpose, focusing all energies on the attainment of that purpose, are able to attract to THEMSELVES people, things and powers that are favorable to accomplishing their purpose.

This is in essence the LAW OF KARMA; the law of CAUSE AND EFFECT; the law of COMPENSATION. We are standing on the threshold of the mental rebirth of the African American consciousness, which includes, *"The Rescue of the Knowledge, the Reconstruction of the Knowledge, and the Re-awakening through the Knowledge."*

May our tapes, seminars, classes, lectures and conferences serve as positive GUIDES on your journey to your *RE-AWAKENING TO SELF EMPOWERMENT THROUGH THE ATTAINMENT OF KNOWLEDGE AND INFORMATION.*

Anthony T. Browder
Author of *From the Browder File*
Director of the Institute of Karmic Guidance

Mr. Browder with his daughter, Atlantis Tye.

About the Author

Anthony T. Browder is a native of Chicago, Illinois and a graduate of Howard University's College of Fine Arts.

He is a single parent, graphic artist, writer, lecturer, independent Egyptologist and cultural historian.

He has lectured throughout the United States, Mexico and Africa, and he has conducted numerous television and radio interviews.

He appeared in a 10 part television series for the program *Spotlight"*, seen Sundays on Channel 32, WHMM-TV in Washington, DC.

Mr. Browder is the founder and director of the *Institute of Karmic Guidance*, a culturally oriented organization which is dedicated to the dissemination of *"Ancient Kemitian (Egyptian) history and metaphysics.'*

One of the most successful endeavors undertaken by the *Institute* was the creation of a speakers bureau, (the *"Free Your Mind"* lecture series) which has sponsored numerous lectures by African American historians, scientists, psychologists and scholars.

Through the *Institute*, Mr. Browder sponsors lectures, seminars, Afrocentric tours of Washington, DC, publishes the *Human Insight* newsletter, conducts monthly study group meetings and annual study tours to Egypt.

He is the author of *From the Browder File: 22 Essays on the African American Experience"* and a frequent contributor to numerous publications.

"Tony" describes himself as a chronicler of facts and information relative to the positive portrayal of the worldwide African experience.

For information on speaking engagements and study tours to Egypt, call or write:

The Institute of Karmic Guidance
PO Box 73025
Washington, DC 20056
(202) 726-0762

VIDEO AND AUDIO TAPE LIST
By Anthony T. Browder

☐ *Ancient Egypt: New Perspectives of an African Civilization* A lecture and slide presentation which features a pictorial and historical overview of ancient Egyptian civilization. Emphasis is placed on the contemporary and historical application of Egyptian philosophy and symbolism.
VHS video tape: $35   Audio tape: $10   Time: 2 hours

☐ *Egyptian Origins of Science and Metaphysics* An introduction to ancient knowledge of the human existence, within the physical realm (Science) and the realm beyond the physical (Metaphysical). This lecture features demonstrations on light and color, and levitation.
VHS video tape: $35   Audio tape: $10   Time: 2 hours

☐ *The African Origins of Christianity* A revealing look at the African influence on religion and the history and symbolic meaning of the bible.
VHS video tape: $35   Audio tape: $10   Time: 2 hours

Spotlight Interviews

☐ A four part series produced by WHMM-TV (Channel 32) at Howard University. Topics include:
  • Overview of Egyptian History and Its Impact on Civilization
  • Egyptian Origins of Science and Metaphysics
  • Afrocentric View of Washington, DC
VHS video tape: $35   Time: 2 hours

Audio Tapes

☐ *The Melanin Report* A review of the "Second Annual Melanin Conference" and a discussion of the physical and spiritual aspects of melanin.
Audio tape: $10   Time: 2½ hours

☐ *African Americans and American History* A discussion of the history of Africans in America, from slavery to the present.
Audio tape: $10   Time: 2½ hours

From the Browder File: 22 Essays on the African American Experience with an Introduction by Asa Hilliard A collection of 22 essays covering a variety of topics relative to the African American experience. This resource guide contains over 90 references, 30 illustrations and 128 pages.
  ☐ Paperback: $9.95
  ☐ Audio Tape: $12.95   Time: 2½ hours

- -

(Please allow 3-4 weeks for delivery)

Name _____   Subtotal_____
Address _____   Shipping & Handling
_____   ($2.50 per item) _____
Telephone # _____   **Total** _____

Please send check or money order to:
The Institute of Karmic Guidance
PO Box 73025 ✿ *Washington, DC   20056* ✿ *(202) 726-0762*

VIDEO AND AUDIO TAPE LIST
By Anthony T. Browder

❑ *Ancient Egypt: New Perspectives of an African Civilization* A lecture and slide presentation which features a pictorial and historical overview of ancient Egyptian civilization. Emphasis is placed on the contemporary and historical application of Egyptian philosophy and symbolism.

VHS video tape: $35   Audio tape: $10   Time: 2 hours

❑ *Egyptian Origins of Science and Metaphysics* An introduction to ancient knowledge of the human existence, within the physical realm (Science) and the realm beyond the physical (Metaphysical). This lecture features demonstrations on light and color, and levitation.

VHS video tape: $35   Audio tape: $10   Time: 2 hours

❑ *The African Origins of Christianity* A revealing look at the African influence on religion and the history and symbolic meaning of the bible.

VHS video tape: $35   Audio tape: $10   Time: 2 hours

Spotlight Interviews

❑ A four part series produced by WHMM-TV (Channel 32) at Howard University. Topics include:

- Overview of Egyptian History and Its Impact on Civilization
- Egyptian Origins of Science and Metaphysics
- Afrocentric View of Washington, DC

VHS video tape: $35   Time: 2 hours

Audio Tapes

❑ *The Melanin Report* A review of the "Second Annual Melanin Conference" and a discussion of the physical and spiritual aspects of melanin.

Audio tape: $10   Time: 2½ hours

❑ *African Americans and American History* A discussion of the history of Africans in America, from slavery to the present.

Audio tape: $10   Time: 2½ hours

From the Browder File: 22 Essays on the African American Experience with an Introduction by Asa Hilliard A collection of 22 essays covering a variety of topics relative to the African American experience. This resource guide contains over 90 references, 30 illustrations and 128 pages.

   ❑ Paperback: $9.95
   ❑ Audio Tape: $12.95   Time: 2½ hours

- -

(Please allow 3-4 weeks for delivery)

Name _____   Subtotal_____

Address _____   Shipping & Handling
_____   ($2.50 per item) _____

Telephone # _____   Total _____

Please send check or money order to:
The Institute of Karmic Guidance
PO Box 73025 ✿ Washington, DC 20056 ✿ (202) 726-0762

This Book
Belong to:

Sister Elder J. Powel
of Wash. DC